Changing Your Self-Concept...
Positive Ways to Deal with Depression, Guilt, Anger, and Fear

Dr. Richard D. Dobbins
VMI Publishers, Sisters, Oregon

Unless otherwise indicated, all Scripture quotations are taken from the Holy Bible, New International Version (NIV), copyright 1973, 1978, 1979 by International Bible Society; Scripture quotations marked NKJV are taken from the New King James Version copyright by Thomas Nelson Publishers. Scripture quotations marked NLT are taken from the New Living Translation, copyright 1996 by Tyndale House Publishers.

Printed in the United States of America

ISBN 0-9712311-5-X

Acknowledgments

I am grateful to all the people responsible for helping me put this book together. My wife has encouraged me to take the time necessary to meet deadlines. She has made invaluable suggestions for improving the book. My secretary, Wandalee Rader, was kind enough to read the manuscript and grammatically edit it. I would also like to express appreciation to my editors and publishers, Bill and Nancie Carmichael, for their creative ideas and patience, urging me to be at my best in this book.

Dedication

This book is dedicated to the many people who have sought my help over the last 35 years. I am indebted to them for many of the discoveries shared with you in this book.

CONTENTS

Introduction

If you are on friendly terms with your feelings it will show on your face. Your countenance reflects your emotional history and how you have chosen to deal with it. All of us go through times when we may appear sad, depressed, angry, guilty, anxious, or confused, but if you are not on friendly terms with your feelings most of the time you are missing out on the joy of life.

Often, while shopping, Priscilla and I will stop to rest on a bench in the mall just to watch people for a few minutes. For us this is great fun. The expressions on some of their faces leave us wondering whether they are finding much joy in life.

A vibrant healthy life expressed through a peaceful and joyful countenance exerts a powerful positive influence upon those around us. As Paul reminds us, "The kingdom of God is not a matter of eating or drinking, but of righteousness, peace, and joy in the Holy Spirit."[1]

Jesus never intended his followers to profess this kingdom without enjoying it. He was not born to bring another religion to the world. He never intended Christianity to become an institution. He presented a way of life He referred to as the Kingdom of God and the Kingdom of heaven.

For many of the people I have seen in counseling, Christianity had become a set of beliefs primarily for escaping hell and going to heaven. Your beliefs are

---

[1] Romans 14:17

important, but a healthy faith is more than a set of beliefs. It is a way of life. It is the celebration of this kingdom of peace and joy!

The spiritual and emotional dimensions of our lives are vitally related. Each impacts upon and interacts with the other in ways that deeply affect the manner in which we experience all other dimensions of life. This book is written to help us understand the nature of this interaction more clearly and to gain better control of it.

Our feelings about ourselves, our families, and life in general are formed very subtly and very early in life—long before we start school. Our spiritual experience grows out of and is affected by these earlier realities.

Mental illness and emotional disturbance not only distort the way we see ourselves and others, but may also distort our view of God and life in general. On the other hand, a healthy spiritual experience can help the mentally ill and emotionally disturbed regain their mental health and deal with life more effectively. When our spiritual experience and religious beliefs are consistent with healthy views of God, self, and others, they help minimize life's pain and maximize its pleasure.

The discussion questions following each chapter are designed to encourage your interaction with what you have just read. An honest transparent response to these will assist you in implementing your insights into a healthier and friendlier relationship with your feelings.

Throughout the book are descriptions of painful problems people have brought to me in counseling. In an effort to help the reader I have shared these experiences. However, the names of the people involved, their circumstances, and other identifying data have been altered so as to protect their confidentiality.

CHAPTER ONE

YOUR FEELINGS: FRIEND OR FOE?

I sensed panic in Andrea's voice as she pleaded over the phone, "Dr. Dobbins, we need your help." "What's wrong?" I asked. "It's Mom, she's flipped out again."

Andrea's mother, Susan, was one of my patients. I said, "Let me talk to her." "You can't," Andrea replied. She's locked herself in the bathroom and she won't come out. We keep pounding on the door and calling to her, but she won't answer. We're afraid she may do something to herself. Could you come over and talk to her? I think she'd listen to you."

I had just sat down to eat dinner with my family, and I didn't want to leave the house if it weren't necessary. So I suggested, "Please tell her I'm on the phone and want to talk to her. See if she will come out of the bathroom to talk with me."

I heard Andrea lay the phone down. I could hear her shout to her mother that I was on the phone and wanted to talk with her. A few seconds later Andrea returned to tell me what I didn't want to hear.

"Dr. Dobbins, Mom didn't respond. What should we do?" "Call 911," I told her. "I'll get there as fast as I can."

From what Andrea had said, I shared her concern about her mother harming herself. I explained the crisis to my family in ways that wouldn't frighten our children, excused myself from the table and sped across town as fast as safety would permit.

By the time I reached their home, the medical

emergency team was already there. They had knocked on
the door and pled for Susan to let them in, but she kept her
silence and refused to give them the satisfaction of knowing she was alive and had heard them.

They quickly took the pins out of the hinges on the
door and we went in. Susan was curled up in a fetal position, totally nude. I asked Andrea to bring a blanket. We
wrapped her mother in it and got Susan to her feet.

Andrea and her brother got into my car and we fol-
lowed the emergency team to the hospital. On the way, I
discovered that Susan's husband, Harry, had gone into
another one of his rages over some trivial issue. This was
not unusual for him.

First he had chased Susan around the dining room
table and then around the kitchen table threatening to beat
her if he caught her. She made it through the hall, up the
stairs and into the bathroom. Having secured the lock, she
fell to the floor in a prenatal position and went into a kind
of catatonic stupor. Temporarily, she had lost her sanity.

Both Harry and Susan are evangelical Christians.
They go to church every Sunday morning and Sunday
night. They never miss Wednesday night prayer meeting.
Harry had gone to Bible college and prided himself in his
disciplined study of Scripture. He was very knowledge-
able about the Bible.

However, that night all Harry's biblical knowledge
was of no practical help in enabling him to control his
temper and Susan's church attendance didn't keep fear
from paralyzing her. Their feelings had become their
biggest foes!

Periodically, Harry and Susan treated their neighbors to these kinds of emotional outbreaks.

People like Harry and Susan have not yet discovered the vital link between their spiritual experience and
their mental health. They may believe all the right things

for staying out of hell and going to heaven, but in the meantime they have little mental peace and even less joy here on earth.

A vibrant, healthy faith is expressed in a celebration of life that is obvious to those around us. "The kingdom of God is not eating and drinking; but righteousness, and peace, and joy in the Holy Spirit"[1]

God made us emotional beings.

The Bible says we are made in the image of God.[2] The Scriptures reveal God to be One who feels as well as thinks.[3] To be made in His image means that we are feeling persons as well as thinking persons.

You and I experience life through our feelings long before we have a vocabulary to express them in our thoughts. Our emotional memories are stored in the amygdala, two almond-like structures that lie just above the brain stem and below the limbic ring in your brain. The feelings stored in our amygdala are what give meaning to our lives.

Intellectual thought must await the acquisition of speech before it can effectually benefit us. The memories generated by thinking are stored in another part of the brain called the neocortex. Memories stored here help you recognize the members of your family. However, the emotional memories of your experience with these people are stored in your amygdala and remind you whether or not you like them.

Unfortunately, life affords us few opportunities to learn how to link these two very different kinds of memories. Consequently, we need help in learning how to define our feelings, label them, talk about them and, if necessary, modify them so we can learn how to live with them as comfortably as possible.

Our emotional history affects our thinking.

When we are young we are taught to pay much more attention to our thoughts than to our feelings. In the early years of life, most of our waking hours are spent in schools primarily dedicated to teaching us how to think. However, we learn to feel at least two years before we have an adequate vocabulary necessary for the simplest forms of thinking. This is why our early emotional history has such a strong influence on the way we begin to verbally describe life to ourselves and others.

Nurturing children through infancy and early childhood is the best investment parents can make in their mental health. Before our children can understand our words they feel our love through our hugs and kisses; they see it in our smiles and hear it in the tone of our voice. Years of clinical experience have convinced me that the lack of nurturance in the preverbal and preschool years of life is the most common contributor to emotional disturbance and mental illness. When one has a vast accumulation of pleasurable memories stored in their amygdala before they learn to talk they are much more likely to develop verbal ways of thinking about life that are enjoyable for themselves and others.

In my formative years no one ever talked to me about my feelings or gave me any instruction in how to translate them into words so I could manage them better and discuss them with others. The only time my feelings were brought to my attention was when my parents or some other adult felt they were inappropriate. Even then, I was not taught what was inappropriate about them or how I could express them more appropriately. Usually, I was just punished for them

The stewardship of our feelings affects all of our relationships. This is true whether we are male or female, young or old, married or single. Becoming aware of our feelings, learning something about their origins, and developing appropriate ways of managing them can enrich our personal life and greatly benefit our interpersonal relationships.

Thank God, feelings can be modified and thoughts can be changed. However, this process does not occur magically or instantaneously. Paul says we are to "put away" the exaggerated and distorted ways in which we store life in our memory when we are children."[4] This requires deliberate and disciplined effort. Defining our feelings and talking about them with someone we trust helps us modify them. Until we do this we cannot change them. This book will explore the spiritual and emotional resources available for such a process. It will introduce you to some practical ideas for changing the way you feel and think about life.

A WHOLESOME FAITH IN GOD

First, we'll look at how a wholesome faith in God enables you to develop and maintain healthy ways of dealing with life in general. Then, over the next five chapters, we will focus on specific problem areas that I have seen many people struggle with again and again in the more than 30 years I have been counseling. These emotional concerns give all of us problems from time to time: our self-image, fear, anger, guilt, and depression.

Self image

Of these, a poor self-image is the most common. Often the roots of this problem can be traced back to improper and/or poorly understood religious training during childhood. This issue is addressed in Chapter 3.

Fear and anxiety

The painful emotions of fear and anxiety also have

their roots in early childhood. In fact, we first experience them in the birth process. I will explain why birth can be so anxiety provoking in Chapter 4. Today, anxiety disorders are one of the most common areas of complaint among adults seen in counseling.

Anger

Anger is particularly difficult for believers to deal with because many of us have been taught that any expression of anger is inconsistent with our faith. Of course, anger doesn't have to present the believer with such an overwhelming predisposition to guilt. It can be a positive, healthy force in his or her life. But it does have to be properly managed. And I'll make some suggestions for doing this in Chapter 5.

Guilt

A healthy conscience and healthy guilt make society possible. However, not all guilt is healthy. Some can be very unhealthy and crippling. There are distinct differences between healthy and unhealthy guilt. In Chapter 6 we'll define some of the important ones. We'll talk about specific ways of identifying and resolving each.

Depression

Depression is the most common of all emotional problems and afflicts an estimated 50 million Americans annually. Many of these are believers. The stress of modern living certainly has contributed to the present epidemic proportions of depression, but it is not new or unique to our generation. In Chapter 7 I will explore ways you can manage bouts with depression. As we will see, depression plagued the lives of many Bible characters.

I have seen many men and women in crisis so depressed that they have tried to take their lives. Many others are troubled by chronic depression whose roots are much more difficult to define. Still others suffer from depression that is more biochemical than circumstantial in nature. But faith in God, coupled with the best information and medical treatment available, can help people deal constructively with these troubled feelings.

The final chapter, "You Can Live in a New Dimension," explains a life-changing process by which we can bring "eternal life" into the problem-solving, decision-making processes of our lives. Some of the most remarkable emotional healings I have ever witnessed—have come through times of private, personal prayer.

As we journey through this book together I hope you will discover practical ways to bring the healing and enabling power of God into your emotional world. May the application of suggestions you find in these pages help you to become a good friend of your feelings!

Discussion Questions

1. In what part of the brain are our emotional memories stored?

2. In what part of the brain are our intellectual memories stored?

3. How do our emotional memories affect our intellectual memories?

4. Are actions more important than words in communicating love? If so, why is this?

5. What five sources of emotional pain do many people share in common?

FOOTNOTES

[1] Romans 14:17
[2] Genesis 1:26-27
[3] Deuteronomy 13:17; Psalms 16:11; John 3:16; Isaiah 55:6-9
[4] Corinthians 13:11

CHAPTER TWO

HOW HEALTHY
IS YOUR FAITH?

For almost an hour, the preacher had been making the brevity of life and the certainty of judgment real to us. As he finished his sermon, with a voice full of emotion he said, "Would everyone here please bow your head and close your eyes? I want to ask you the most important question of your life."

Then he began what anyone who has ever been to a Christian evangelistic service recognizes as the invitation. "If you were to die right now are you absolutely sure you would go to heaven?" he asked.

Now, I knew I wasn't the world's greatest sinner, but I wasn't involved in church and I was doing and saying many things that were contrary to what my church and family had taught me. My mother had become so concerned about the spiritual direction of my life that she had asked a young lady who had caught my eye if she would invite me to church. This is why I was there.

However, that night an additional load of guilt fell on me for I had been involving this young lady (who had since become my girlfriend) in the kinds of activities both of us had been taught were wrong. My resistance to the preacher's appeal broke when she reached over to return my high school class ring, which I had given her as a token of my love for her. As she handed my ring back to me she gave me an ultimatum. "Unless you become a Christian I can't continue to go with you." I will never forget those words.

When that kind of leverage was added to the guilt I

was feeling already, it was enough to send me to the altar. With the help of some friends I prayed the sinner's prayer. God forgave me.

I remember leaving church that night feeling so clean. I felt like a great weight had been lifted from my shoulders. It was like I was beginning life all over again! Everyone rejoiced with me because I had given my life to Christ.

I still look back on that decision as the wisest in my life, but now I understand that there were many other factors besides the pastor's sermon and yielding to Christ's claim on my life involved in sending me to the altar that night. This decision not only resolved my major conflict with sin, it also relieved tension between me and my family, reconciled me to my girlfriend, and gave me the spiritual resources that I would need for coming to terms with the many pains from my highly complicated past.

To this day, I am unsure which of these pressures the Holy Spirit used most to influence my decision for Christ. I don't know whether I went to the altar for salvation or "gal-vation," but I do know that God changed my life that night.

This is how tightly the spiritual, emotional, and social issues of life are intertwined. And today, more and more, professionals from the fields of religion and the behavioral sciences are beginning to understand this.

When I began my walk with God as a teenager my mental health was not one of my major concerns. At that time, I was so idealistic in my faith I simply didn't understand how devout Christians could have any emotional problems. And I certainly wasn't alone in this conviction.

After all, didn't the Scriptures say that when we accept Christ as our Savior old things would pass away and all things would become new?[1] A literal interpretation of this passage expresses the prevailing belief in our

church and many others at the time. That is, we believed
that when we became a Christian everything about us was
totally, miraculously and instantaneously changed and any
negative impact our personal history may have had on our
mental and social health was completely cancelled.

Our church believed the conversion experience not
only completely healed us from our past, but also transformed our history, and protected us from any future consequences of it. Regardless of how destructive our early
home life might have been or how foolish the decisions
we made in our past may have been, once we accepted
Jesus Christ as our Savior we could look forward to the
same kind of future that a person would have who grew up
in an emotionally healthy home and made wise decisions
all of his life.

All we had to do to lead a trouble-free life was to
read the Bible and pray every day like we should. If we
did these things we would never have any painful emotional problems and nothing devastating would ever happen to us. This was frequently implied from the pulpit
and often openly taught. And I believed what I was
taught.

Today, I understand more clearly what Paul was
saying to the Corinthian church. The Greek construction
used in 2 Corinthians 5:17 made it clear that becoming a
new creature in Christ was an initial experience in a
process. That is, once a person becomes a Christian "old
things" begin to, and keep on passing away. "All things"
begin to and keep on becoming new.

In reality, there may be destructive consequences
of many unwise decisions we have made in our past that
will accompany us into our new life in Christ. For example, suppose a person has been foolish enough to mother
or father a child before marriage. Will accepting Christ as
his or her Savior spare them the painful consequences of

those actions? No. This person will still have to deal with all of the issues that flow out of being a single mom or dad, or the memories of giving the child up for adoption, or even worse, the long-term affects of an abortion.

The decisions we make in life, good and bad, are like seeds we plant in the soil of our future. Once we have made them they inevitably grow to bless or curse us by their harvest.[2] Remember, there are four laws of the harvest:

1. If we don't sow we won't reap.
2. If we sow we will reap.
3. If we sow we will reap what we sow.
4. If we sow we will reap more than we sow.

These laws bless us with the consequences of our good decisions and painfully plague us with the consequences of our bad ones.

We also have to deal with the tragic consequences of accidents, illnesses, natural disasters and others' foolish choices. As Christians, God gives us the power of His grace and the wisdom of Scripture to help us deal with these realities, but we are not exempt from them.

It would be many years before I would come to this understanding of my faith. However, at the time of my conversion I was under the influence of a tragically oversimplistic view of the Christian life.

Both of my parents had been active in church all my life. I assumed I had grown up in a normal emotionally healthy Christian family. At least, none of us had ever had to go for counseling. The way people in our church who went for counseling were whispered about left no doubt in my mind that something was missing in their walk with God. I believed that anyone we met at church who had been genuinely saved was bound to be emotionally healthy. After all, how could anyone be a sincere Christian and have serious emotional problems?

Years later, when I looked back on these early years I realized I brought into my Christian life many unresolved mental health issues from my family's history. I also began to recognize major mental health problems in other members of my family who were Christians. But at the time of my conversion my naivety kept me completely unaware that anyone in our family had any emotional problems.

Faith in Christ helps you deal with your past.

By the time each of us reaches adulthood we have accumulated a history of hurts and habits. When we accept Jesus Christ as our personal Savior these do not magically disappear. God does not want us to be prisoners of our past, nor does He want us to feel we have to deny these hurts and habits in order to please Him.

He has provided grace that can bring healing to these destructive chapters of our past through a prayerful application of His Word. The Bible refers to this process as "sanctification."[3] We will talk more about this in later chapters.

Unhealthy faith—unhealthy feelings

In the past, ministers and psychologists tended to view their respective fields as antithetical—like oil and water. According to them, religion and psychology just didn't mix. Some still feel that way.

Today, however, there is evidence that an increasing number of reputable people from both camps are looking at their old viewpoint with a more careful eye. They are beginning to see the benefit of helping the minister better understand the emotional issues involved in a person's religious experience, and of helping the psychologist or psychiatrist better understand the spiritual issues involved in a person's emotional life.

The issues of our faith are much more important to us than the psychological issues of life because our faith affects us eternally. Nevertheless, we need all the help both fields can provide in our effort to stay mentally healthy in our sick society.

Myrtle's story

The intertwining nature of the spiritual and emotional issues of life became real to Myrtle and her family through her painful mental health crisis.

One day she came home from a prayer meeting and announced to her husband, George, that Jesus was calling her into a special life of prayer. He didn't understand exactly what that meant.

However, within a few days, George began to notice that Myrtle was starting to neglect their home. She had been an immaculate housekeeper. Now, when he came home from work in the evening, the dishes from breakfast were still on the table. The beds weren't made. Their two boys, ages five and seven, obviously had been allowed to run through the house all day as they pleased. None of these things seemed to bother Myrtle any more.

When George brought these things to her attention, she cried and complained that he just didn't understand her longing for God. She lamented over his lack of spiritual commitment.

An unhealthy religious experience not only opens the way to a misguided faith, it can also be detrimental to your mental health. George was finding this out. Myrtle was developing obvious symptoms of a serious mental health problem.

Soon she began sleeping in another bedroom so she wouldn't awaken him when she got up to pray early in the morning. Of course, that also made it easier for her to avoid what she called George's "carnal advances."

George knew something was happening to his wife, but he didn't know what it was or what to do about it. Finally, he talked to the minister in charge of the prayer meeting Myrtle had been attending. The minister agreed that her actions were strange; however, he attributed her behavior to the fact that spiritual experience was a relatively new thing for Myrtle. He encouraged George to be patient and assured him that his wife's rather fanatical emphasis on prayer would soon level off. The minister promised to have a talk with Myrtle.

He talked to her right away, but it didn't seem to help. Instead, she took offense at what the minister said and chided him for not being more spiritual. She began to get up even earlier in the morning for prayer.

One morning George discovered she was waking their sons at five o'clock in the morning to pray with her before they left for school. When he asked why she was doing this, she calmly told him Jesus had appeared to her in a vision. He had told her to include the boys in her early morning prayer, because He was calling them to be ministers.

At this point, George made a wise but difficult decision. He sought professional help for Myrtle. At first, she wanted nothing to do with psychiatric help. Only when her husband convinced her that the people at our center would understand her faith did she agree to see me.

I never will forget my first session with Myrtle. She was very eager to see if I would pass her orthodoxy test. She wanted to know if Jesus was real to me. She asked me if I believed the Bible was infallible. I assured her I did. She asked me if Jesus Christ was my personal Savior. I told her He was. She asked me if I believed in the supernatural. I told her I did. Being assured by these answers, she told me about her own encounter with Christ in great detail. Of course, for her this experience was very real even though it had been very disintegrative and disabling for her.

Healthy faith integrates you.

A healthy religious experience is never disintegrative. It is never disabling. In fact, just the opposite is true. It is always integrative. It always enables us to function better. In Myrtle's case, a healthy religious experience would have helped her function more effectively as a wife, mother and homemaker. But, to a trained observer, the disintegrative nature of her spiritual experience marked it as being very unhealthy.

Taking great pains to reinforce the healthy parts of her faith, I assured Myrtle that although her symptoms were religious, her problem was emotional. I asked if she had recently experienced some emotional shock or major personal loss. She confided in me that her father had died recently and her best friend had been killed in a tragic automobile accident about six months prior to the time she came to see me. Myrtle was overwhelmed by these losses. It is impossible for a healthy person to suffer the deaths of two important people in their world and not be emotionally affected in some way.

I suggested to George that it would be helpful if the boys could be cared for by another member of the family for a few weeks while his wife got the help she needed. Myrtle was hospitalized. During her five-week hospital stay, she was given a combination of medicine, biblical counseling and rest. Under these conditions and the supervision of our staff psychiatrist, Myrtle made good progress toward recovery.

After she was released from the hospital, she and George resumed their life together as they had known it before. Gradually, Myrtle regained her ability to care for their two healthy boys and their home. I continued to see her for counseling until she had worked through her grief and learned new, healthy ways of applying her faith to her daily life experiences. I helped her learn how to tell the difference between a healthy and an unhealthy religious experience so she didn't need to be afraid of her faith—or fear that the nightmare of her emotional disturbance would return.

Not all forms of Christianity are emotionally healthy.

Sick forms of the Christian religion have been around for 2000 years. John writes about immature believers who are overwhelmed with fear and insecurity.[4] Paul warns believers about Christian teachers who prey upon spiritually immature and emotionally unhealthy Christians through "cunning, craftiness and deceitful scheming."[5]

Is there a way to tell the difference between healthy and unhealthy religious experiences? Yes God has provided the biblical guidelines we need for differentiating between healthy and unhealthy religious experiences. This is why it is so important to know the Scriptures well enough to recognize when they are being interpreted in ways contrary to our mental health.

We need biblical ways of testing religious ideas and experiences before we open ourselves to them. Often, in our mass-media world, we are confronted with many sick forms of religion that are made to appear quite appealing. But Paul warns us to carefully weigh the words of anyone who is trying to spiritually influence us.[6] As we listen to people speak to us from the Scriptures we need practical ways of determining how biblically sound and healthy their teachings are.

TEN WAYS TO TEST YOUR FAITH

Many of the emotionally troubled people who come to our center for help are suffering from symptoms brought on by unhealthy religious beliefs. From years of clinical experience with such people I have defined some biblical guidelines for helping a person discern the difference between a healthy faith and one that is unhealthy.

Applying the following guidelines to your faith can spare you the pain and confusion of an unhealthy faith, and help you reap all the benefits of a healthy faith.

1. Healthy faith is affirmed in fellowship.

Beware of isolated religious groups who insist on rigid conformity to strange beliefs and practices that have little biblical support. Remember, Paul admonished Timothy to apply reputable scholarship in his approach to biblical interpretations so that he could "rightly" divide the Word of truth.[7] Also, Peter warns that no passage of Scripture should be lifted out of its context and interpreted alone.[8] Being aware of what precedes and follows is essential to a correct understanding of the passage. What the Bible says about the subject in other places is also important.

Christianity embraces a wide variety of groups that are identified by their honest differences. These are distinguished from each other by different scholarly interpretations of portions of the Bible. If our faith is healthy, we should be able to identify theologically with at least one of these groups. When a person's beliefs are so unique and different that he is unable to find any group with whom he is comfortable, his beliefs should be held suspect. Remember, Jesus wants His followers to be one with Him and with one another.[9]

2. Healthy faith sees God as love.

None of us relate to God as He is. We relate to Him as we picture Him in our minds. Many still see Him as angry. They feel His approval is beyond their reach so

they content themselves with trying desperately to avoid
His wrath. They are unaware of God's constant care for
them. We'll see how this affects a believer's other relationships later on when we discuss, "Anger: Master or
Servant?"

Often, when people view God as angry and wrath-
ful, they are placing too strong an emphasis on an Old
Testament view of God. This is why they see Him as an
angry judge. And, it's true . . . God did preside over the
flood, the destruction of wickedness in Sodom and
Gomorrah, and the expulsion of the Canaanites.[10] But He
is also the loving God who provided us with the birth of
His only begotten Son, Jesus Christ.[11]

Each of us forms our mental picture of God
between our fifth and seventh year. Our relationship with
our earthly parents tends to strongly influence our image
of God. After we come to know Christ, we should be sure
our image of God is consistent with the loving nature of
Jesus.

This becomes obvious from the interchange Philip
had with Jesus. "Lord, show us the Father, and that will
be enough for us." Jesus replies, "Don't you know me,
Philip, even after I have been among you such a long
time? Anyone who has seen me has seen the Father."[12]
So, when Christians wonder what God is like, we are to
think of Jesus.

3. Healthy faith fosters self-worth.

No other religion in the world places as much
value on an individual as does the Christian faith. Jesus
declares that if it were possible to gain the whole world in
exchange for your own soul, what you lost would be
worth more than what you gained.[13] What a statement of
individual worth! And it is the payment of Christ's blood
as the price of our redemption that attributes such worth to

every human being.[14]

Every human being is a sinner.[15] And the Scriptures insist that we are honest about our sins—with God and ourselves. John says that when we say we have no sin we deceive ourselves.[16] But, in spite of our sins, God loves us. Paul says God not only loves us when we become His children, He loved us while we were His enemies.[17] Confession of our sin should lead us to the peace and joy of forgiveness.[18] Discovering God's love can make a world of difference in how you view yourself. It also deeply affects the way you feel about God

4. Healthy faith meets reality.

What is reality? At any given moment, reality for each of us is a personal combination of past influences, present stresses, and their interactions with each other. These influences and stresses are fourfold in nature: physical, psychological, social and spiritual.

Under stress these dimensions of reality tend to impact each other. For example, in our culture we expect men to be taller than women. So, a man who is genetically determined to be short or a woman who inherits her family's height will experience emotional and social stress as a result of this physical factor in his or her life.

Being born into poverty or wealth is a social fact of life over which we have no control. However, such an event can have a profound effect on the physical, psychological, and spiritual dimensions of one's life.

The sudden loss of a loved one, or your wealth or your job can trigger a serious depression. This kind of situational depression can drastically affect the physical, social and even spiritual dimension of life.

Obviously, most of us bring into our *present,* memories of events and experiences from our past that could adversely affect our mental health. All of us face the risk of stresses from our present that can devastate us. Life holds no guarantee of protection for any of us. There is no life without storms.

Jesus makes this clear in the closing illustration of His Sermon on the Mount. He predicts disaster for those who hear His teachings but do not apply them to life, but guarantees the survival of those who respond to life's storms in ways He has taught them.[19]

Each of us creates a story about our storms!

At times, life deals potentially crippling blows to each of us. But what happens to us is not nearly as critical to our emotional and spiritual health as the way we choose to interpret and react to what happens. Solomon wisely observed this when he wrote, "For as he thinks in his heart, so is he."[20] Each of us uniquely perceives his or her circumstances in life and responds to them. This is what accounts for the different ways people who grow up in the same home are affected by their family history. Listening to individual members of some families talk about how they were raised often leaves you feeling that they grew up in different homes.

In my work as a therapist I try to make it very clear to the hurting people seeing me that no one lives with the facts of their past. Each of us lives with our interpretation of those facts. And, although no one can change what has happened to them they can be helped to find a different way of feeling and thinking about what has happened to them, a way that won't hurt as much as the way they are currently viewing these things. Of course, each person must be willing to work at making this discovery.

5. Healthy faith prepares you for the future.

The current rate of technological change is mind-boggling. Advances in science, technology, and industry have brought to us such rapid means of transportation and communication that we are exposed to as many life experiences in a year as previous generations knew in a lifetime. Consequently, we stagger under the impact of information and stimulation overload.

For example, many of us travel 20 miles to work each day. After a round trip of 40 miles and working eight hours, we may go out with family or friends for an evening of entertainment. Back at the beginning of the twentieth century, however, just traveling 40 miles would have consumed the entire day.

Then, Americans traveled by sailing ships, horses and buggies and covered wagons. These limited means of transportation allowed the boundaries of oceans, mountains and rivers to separate and protect people. Today, we travel by cars, trains, airplanes and space shuttles. The natural barriers of rivers, mountains, deserts and oceans no longer offer us any protection from what is happening in other parts of our world.

We have also had to adapt to rapidly changing methods of communication: newspapers, radio, television, computers, modems, e-mail, cell phones, fax, and video-conferencing. Today, we live in a global village where it is impossible to be sheltered from what is happening in the rest of the world. What happens on one part of our planet immediately impacts the people of every other part.

In the face of this unbelievable acceleration of change, many people are struggling with crippling levels of tension, worry, and anxiety.

Healthy faith is expressed in flexibility.

Some forms of religious orthodoxy are character-ized by a style of thinking which is rigid and inflexible. People who hold to this kind of belief are uncomfortable in the face of change. In fact, they take pride in their intransigence. They resist being inundated with informa-tion overload by trying desperately to deny the daily reali-ties of their world, standing firmly on the conviction that they must not change.

Listening to them, you would think that the less a person changes, the more like God he is. In defense of their resistance to change, these people often quote, "For I am the Lord, I change not."[21] They emphasize that, "Jesus Christ is the same yesterday and today and forever."[22]

I have talked to many Christians victimized by this kind of teaching. I have tried to help them become more flexible in their thinking by suggesting that because none of us are God or Jesus, we cannot afford the luxury of remaining the same. We must be open to change. And, a healthy faith can help you adapt to it.

Of course, it is healthy to fear any change that would compromise our relationship with Jesus Christ. Sometimes the graduate students in our counseling classes experience this kind of fear. They are afraid of changes that occur as a result of the intellectual challenge and self-examination graduate studies demand. They have to be reassured that a healthy faith can accommodate a growing person.

I understand their dilemma because I grew up in a religious environment that taught me to be suspicious of change. I experienced that same kind of anxiety when I was stretching and growing out of some of the unhealthy ideas of my early faith. So I share with my students a statement God helped me define for my own reassurance at that time in my life:

"To live is to grow. To grow is to change. If one cannot discern the difference between the change that results from growth and the change that results from the loss of one's faith, his fear of losing his faith makes him resist all change. Then his faith becomes an inhibitor of, rather than a facilitator of, his growth."

Take a few minutes to reflect on this statement. Do you know of anything that is living that isn't growing in some way? Do you know of anything that is growing that isn't changing?

It is never God's will for our faith to get in the way of our growth. Healthy growth never increases the distance between God and us. It lessens it. The more we learn about life, the more in awe of God we stand. Our love for God grows greater and we are seized by a more intense desire to know Him.

6. Healthy faith helps you manage stress and anxiety.

The stress and anxiety of our fast-paced world do not have to be destructive. Dr. Hans Selye, world-renowned specialist on stress, coined the word "eustress" to describe how the energy created by stress can be converted into productive, creative activities.[23]

Not only is it unrealistic for us to expect to live totally free of stress and anxiety, it is probably impossible. In fact, certain amounts of both stress and anxiety are creatively related to times of excitement, motivation, and growth in life.

Think how boring life would be without these moments. A little test anxiety motivates the student to study more, which usually results in a better grade. Entertainers and athletes expect to feel some tension and anxiety just before they go into action. It helps them perform better.

However, long, unrelenting periods of tension and anxiety can cripple a person. Under certain circumstances, the phobic person is literally paralyzed by anxiety. And I have seen people so overwhelmed by fear that they are unable to leave the security of their home without a family member or friend accompanying them.

The fear of doing a less-than-perfect job keeps many obsessive-compulsive people from finishing any of the tasks they start. A person suffering from an obsessive fear of dirt or germs may wash her hands 50 to 100 times a day in an effort to be germ free.

Many people—including Christians—suffer from these or other forms of illness due largely to anxiety. It doesn't have to be this way. As you learn to order your life according to the teachings of Jesus, the tensions and anxieties of life become more manageable. After all, He taught us not to worry about material things, but to put the kingdom of God first in our lives and trust Him to see that our material needs are met.[24]

Most of our worries are related to our physical existence. And most of them never materialize. You would think that fact in itself would discourage people from worrying. And yet, for many it only tends to reinforce worrying.

If you want to test this, try a little experiment with a group of your friends. Give them a sheet of paper with the following instructions, "On the front side of this sheet of paper list all the things you have worried about during this past year." After they have finished this task, further instruct them to, "Turn the paper over and list on the back all of these things you worried about which actually happened." They will be surprised at how few of the things they worried about actually happened.

When our faith is healthy, we trust more and worry less. God wants us to be good stewards of our possessions, but none of them is worthy of our anxiety. All of them perish with use. That is why the healthy believer learns to be more concerned about spiritual matters and less concerned with material things.

7. Healthy faith finds joy in giving.

Giving grudgingly doesn't bless anyone. Unselfish giving brings joy. This spiritual principle has to be experienced before one can believe it. "Try it—you'll like it." This is what the prophet Malachi says, "Test me in this," says the Lord Almighty, "and see if I will not throw open the floodgates of heaven, and pour out so much blessing that you will not have enough room for it."[25]

Giving is contrary to our selfish human nature. We tend to think the greater joy is in receiving. And yet, when parents compare the Christmas memories of their childhood and the joy of having received from their parents with the joys of giving to their own children, there's no question which memories are more joyful. Seeing the happiness that one's giving brings to those who receive is the greater joy by far.

And there are so many ways we can give. Here are just a few: taking the time to listen to a friend pour out his or her pain to you; reading a story to your children or grandchildren; involving yourself in church and community service. These are all forms of giving. And each of them yields its own unique joy.

In giving, we become a part of the people to whom we give. We are represented in whatever their life and ministry become. It is in giving that each of us shares in the harvest of another's life. Once this discovery is made, we no longer give grudgingly or out of necessity. We give from the heart, knowing that "God loves a cheerful giver."[26]

8. Healthy faith manages anger constructively.

No one lives without anger. You may be so threatened by anger that you learn ways of hiding it from yourself. You may even deny it. Nevertheless, you still experience it.

Over a long period of time, hidden anger can be very damaging. If you impulsively act out your anger, you take unnecessary risks that often complicate your life. If you displace your anger—if you express it toward someone you fear less than the person who provoked it— you are likely to damage important relationships in your life.

You are wiser to think of anger as unexpressed energy. This allows you to understand anger management as energy management. Finding constructive ways to put that energy to work is the secret of making anger your friend instead of your enemy.

The energy generated by anger can cut grass, scrub floors, drive golf balls, wash walls, and do many other things. Why not put your anger to work for you? It makes a great servant, but a poor master. Later in this book I will give you a formula for managing anger that has helped many people make a friend of their anger.

9. Healthy faith balances work and play.

Both work and play are important issues in emotional health. The key is balance. Somewhere between "workaholics" and "couch potatoes" there is a blend that is right for you.

Many people are surprised to find out that work is not a part of the curse. When God made man, He gave him a job. Work is essential to health—both physically demanding work and intellectual work. God gave Adam the physical task of dressing and caring for the Garden of Eden. He also brought all the animals to Adam and gave him the intellectual task of naming them. We need to work with our bodies and our minds.

We spend more time at work than in any other waking activity. This is why it is so important for young people to give careful thought to the kind of work they are gifted to do and would like to do so they can prepare themselves for it. They should have some definite ideas about where they think they would fit best in the work world by the time they are ready for high school. Looking forward to earning your living doing something you really enjoy doing is a pleasure few people know.

As important as work is, we must also remember that God made us to play. One day in seven He designed for worship, rest, and recreation. Healthy people are never too busy to enjoy playing.

When I was a child, the fourth commandment which says we should keep the Sabbath holy, was interpreted to mean, "You can't have any fun on Sunday." There was no play of any kind permitted. I dreaded Sundays. Don't misunderstand me—I believe worship is the most important activity of the Lord's Day and should have priority over other activities. However, I also believe Sunday is a day for family and recreation. When this balance is kept, children learn to love worship and adults remember how to play.

Not only is play important to a healthy life, so is a sense of humor. Both of these help you avoid the misery of circumstantial depression—the kind that results from a person being overwhelmed by life.

10. Healthy faith loves and forgives others.

Paul reminded Timothy that "God has not given us the spirit of timidity; but a spirit of power, of love, and of self-discipline."[27] Notice that love is the second gift mentioned. Power is the first. No one can express true love from a position of weakness.

Jesus came to love His enemies and to lay down his life for them. He was able to manifest this kind of love because He knew that once his enemies had taken his life from Him, His Heavenly Father would give Him the power to take it up again. Remember, Jesus said, "No one takes [my life] from me, but I lay it down of my own accord. I have authority to lay it down, and I have authority to take it again."[28]

Often, I see people trying to live the Christian life by sheer willpower simply because they believe this is their Christian duty. Sometimes I refer to this as the "Boy Scout" approach to the Christian life. Remember their motto? "On my honor I will do my best to do my duty to God and my country." What a frustrating experience this must be! In living the Christian life our will is important, but it is not adequate for this task. As Christians we are commanded to love everyone Christ died for. This includes our enemies. Without God's divine enablement it is impossible for you and me to do this."[29]

As God enables you to love and forgive, recognize the supernatural dimension of these gifts. Celebrate them! Express them! As you do, your ability to love and forgive will expand to include not only your family and friends but also your enemies. Being able to love and forgive leaves your tomorrows free from the anger, fear and bitterness of your yesterdays.

Remember, even in our crazy, mixed-up world, you can enjoy the best of mental health. Your faith is an important part of all this. Keep it healthy. A healthy faith will enable you to avoid unnecessary mental health risks, support you in the unavoidable storms of life, and help you celebrate life more joyfully when things goes well.

Over the next few pages you will discover how vitally your faith is related to your self-image.

Discussion Questions

1. In what ways is life more complex today than when our grandparents and parents were children?

2. Identify some socially popular activities that are unhealthy.

3. Identify and discuss ways in which a person's faith and emotional health affect each other.

4. How does a person's emotional health enhance his/her faith?

5. How does a healthy faith help a person deal with mental health problems?

6. If all changes are not for one's good, how does a person know which changes to resist and which ones to accept?

7. Discuss the kinds of differences a person might accept without fearing they were compromising his/her faith.

8. Define some cultural and social changes that a Christian should not accept.

9. What kinds of changes would Saul of Tarsus have resisted that Paul the Apostle felt he could accept?

10. Does mature love flow from weakness or strength? Explain.

FOOTNOTES

[1] 2 Corinthians 5;17
[2] Galations 6:7-9
[3] John 17:17-19; 1 Thessalonians 4:3-4
[4] 1 John 4:18
[5] Ephesians 4:14
[6] 1 Corinthians 14:29; Hebrews 5:12-13
[7] 2 Timothy 2:15
[8] 2 Peter 1:20
[9] John 17:21
[10] Genesis 7:5-24; 19:1-29; Joshua 24:1-13
[11] John 3:16-17
[12] John 14:9
[13] Mark 8:36-37
[14] 1 Peter 1:18-19
[15] Romans 3:23
[16] 1 John 1:8
[17] Romans 5:6-9
[18] 1 John 1:9
[19] Matthew 7:24-27
[20] Proverbs 23:7
[21] Malachi 3:6
[22] Hebrews 13:8
[23] Arlen, Gary. **Eusress in the Always-on Crowd.** Find Articles.com 12/20/2001
[24] Matthew 6:28-34
[25] Malachi 3:10-12
[26] 2 Corinthians 9:7
[27] 2 Timothy 1:7
[28] John 10:17-18
[29] Matthew 5:43-48

CHAPTER THREE

YOU CAN CHANGE
YOUR SELF-CONCEPT

F inally, Jerry's passivity had driven him and Sue into marriage counseling. In this first session Sue was seething over having to assume so much responsibility for the family. The scowl on her face and the glare from her eyes eloquently communicated Sue's anger and frustration as she exclaimed, "Oh, fine Jerry! Sure! Whether it's planning our social life, disciplining our children, or managing the family budget, I'm the one who always gets stuck with it. You seem to think you can just go along for the ride. Well, I've taken it for 13 years, but I can tell you one thing, Jerry, I've had it! If things don't change, I'm out of here."

I didn't see how Jerry could sit there so quietly and absorb all of Sue's verbal barrages without saying a word. So, finally I asked, "What about that, Jerry?"

"She's right," he agreed. "That's the way it's been." This brief exchange proved to be an eloquent example of their pattern of communication.

Jerry's typical response to Sue's agitation was silence. Her way of reacting to his passivity was to verbally attack him while withdrawing emotionally and sexually from him. Their love life had dwindled to almost nothing. It never had been good. Jerry lacked passion. Sue lacked desire. In all their years of marriage, she had never been orgasmic.

Early in my work with them I realized how aggravating Jerry's "silent treatment" could be for Sue. As you might imagine, she was the talkative one in our sessions. However, when Jerry did volunteer a comment I was impressed with his insight and judgment. I remember saying to him, "Jerry, when you do manage to enter into the conversation with Sue, your remarks are very helpful and she seems to receive them well. Why don't you talk more?"

I was surprised to see his eyes fill with tears as he replied, "I guess it's because when I was growing up as a kid nobody at home seemed to care what I thought about anything. At our house, kids were to be 'seen and not heard.' I guess I've just grown up believing that no one else was interested in my opinions so it was best to keep them to myself."

From this little bit of conversation Jerry's destructive view of himself was obvious. I realized I would have to spend some time alone with him helping to correct the seriously mistaken ideas he had about himself and how others saw him.

Jerry responded well to the times we had together. As a result, he finally began to understand that he was not dumb. He discovered how important his opinions could be to the success of his marriage and began to work very hard at appropriately expressing them to Sue.

Over the ensuing weeks Jerry's behavior changed...rather dramatically. He assumed more responsibility for their financial obligations and the everyday tasks of the home. He became more assertive in his communications with Sue and more attentive to their children. She no longer had to bear the burden of Jerry's passivity.

Sue had always loved Jerry. Now, her respect for him began to grow. All these changes brought the spark back into their love life. With the help of a more assertive partner, Sue became more responsive to Jerry's passion and eventually found orgasmic delight in their physical intimacy. This new dimension of pleasure intensified the love bond between them. Obviously, they no longer needed my help.

I can't help wondering how many other people are just like Jerry. With a little help in changing the way they see themselves, they could get much more out of life and contribute much more to their marriage and family. And only God knows what a difference their increased joy in living would mean to the credibility of their Christian testimony.

Many Christians lack healthy feelings about themselves.

There is no biblical guarantee that you will automatically receive healthy feelings about yourself when you accept Jesus as your Savior. Some do. But many do not.

In fact, some Christians believe that to have good feelings about one's self is to be proud and conceited. Because God despises both of these traits they resist any effort to develop healthy feelings of self-worth. They defend their sense of worthlessness as the only biblical way to see themselves.[1] Often, such believers are totally unaware of how much they reek with spiritual pride.

Unworthy . . . but NOT worthless

I believe much of the confusion over the way God wants us to think of ourselves can be cleared up by understanding the difference between being unworthy and being worthless. The word "unworthy" means undeserving. In view of the price God paid to make us His children we all are unworthy. Who can be worthy of Calvary? We all are undeserving of God's love.

On the other hand, "worth" relates to value established in the marketplace. When Jesus asks what a person will profit from gaining the whole world if in the process he loses himself He is making a statement of human worth. The obvious inference is that what a person loses in such an exchange (himself) is worth more in God's sight than what the person gained (the whole world).[2]

The price of our redemption establishes our worth.

God loved us so much that He was willing to redeem us (buy us back from sin and death) by giving the life of His sinless Son to "atone" for our sins.[3] Both Paul and Peter reveal this unthinkable price God paid to make us His children.[4]

How can anyone for whom such a price was paid think if himself or herself as being worthless. No human being is worthy of such a divine sacrifice. Nonetheless, because of that sacrifice no human being is worthless . . . without value. The death of Jesus Christ attributes immeasurable worth to each of us.

This discovery is life changing.

A person who discovers the worth God ascribes to him or her in Jesus is neither proud nor conceited. They are humbled to find that such a price was paid for their redemption.

Calvary establishes the worth of every human being. It gives to each of us a value that cannot be expressed in material terms. With this discovery comes a renewed sense of meaning to one's life and a desire to share this good news with others who still see themselves as worthless and their lives without meaning.

God's Word gives us many proven prescriptions for achieving and maintaining a healthy self-image. However, prescriptions are powerless unless the medicine is taken according to directions. The truth of Scripture has to be applied if the benefits are to be enjoyed.

When Jerry put God's Word into action in his life he saw himself, his marriage, and his relationship to his family in a different light. What happened to Jerry can happen to anyone . . . it can happen to you! You can learn to have healthy feelings about yourself.

We were created to be feeling and thinking persons.

The Bible tells us we are made in God's image.[5] What does this mean? It means we are feeling persons as well as thinking persons because God not only thinks, he also feels.

The Scriptures frequently refer to God's feelings as well as His thoughts. Since we are made in His image you and I experience life not just through our thoughts, but also through our feelings.

In fact, during the first two or three years of life, before we learn to talk, our world is almost entirely one of feeling. People, animals, and things are identified by the varying degrees of pleasure or pain they bring to us. We become attached to those that bring us more pleasure than pain, and frightened of those who bring us more pain than pleasure.

Long before a baby can talk he has unmistakable non-verbal ways of clearly identifying those people, animals, and objects that are sources of pleasure or pain for him. Parents have no difficulty understanding these feelings. Only as we acquire a vocabulary do we become thinking persons. Initially our words simply become the means of intellectually describing to ourselves the ways we have already learned to feel about the people, animals, and objects in our world.

We learn to identify our world emotionally two or three years before we can describe it to ourselves even in the crude and inaccurate language of early childhood. Nevertheless, in spite of the fact that our use of words is initially influenced greatly by our emotions, our culture teaches us much more about the thinking side of life than it does about the feeling side.

For example, public education is devoted almost entirely to teaching us how to think. Recall your school days. If they were like mine, you were given far more opportunities to learn how to live with your thoughts than how to live with your feelings. How sad this is.

Most of our enjoyment in life will flow out of our relationships with people. These relationships are discovered and developed through emotional skills we have learned that keep us in touch with our own feelings as well as those we generate in others. Without these skills a person is handicapped in their ability to build and maintain mutually satisfying relationships with others.

Our personal happiness is greatly affected by the skills we develop in discovering and defining our feelings about ourselves and others. If a person cannot identify his feelings and articulate them he cannot modify them. On the other hand, identifying the feelings you have about yourself and others and talking about them with someone you trust can help you modify those feelings. This is what happens in counseling. Perhaps this is why men generally have more difficulty benefiting from counseling than women. What makes it so difficult for men to share their feelings with others?

Boys and girls learn different ways to deal with feelings.
Parents are more likely to talk to their little girls about emotions than they are to their little boys . . . except for anger. In most homes the verbalization of feelings is de-emphasized if not discouraged for boys. This makes boys more likely to be oblivious to their own emotions and less aware of the feelings of others.[6]

Girls develop language skills more quickly than boys. So, they learn to articulate their feelings earlier and better than boys. Such a disparity in managing emotions widens the gap between males and females as they grow into adolescence.

This is experienced in the ways boys and girls relate to their peers. Girls tend to cluster in small intimate groups held together by cooperation. Boys tend to form larger groups within which competition becomes important.

When a girl in the group gets hurt and cries, the other girls come to her assistance. When a boy gets hurt he resists crying for fear of being called a "sissy." Boys take pride in being tough-minded and independent. They tend to be threatened by anything that challenges their independence. On the other hand, girls prefer to be part of a web of connectedness with other girls and are more likely to be disturbed by breakups in their friendships with these girls. So, by the time men and women enter marriage they are in two very different emotional worlds.

Most of us learn too late in life that the way we deal with our feelings affects all of our relationships . . . including our relationship with our self. Misunderstandings between mates, friction between parents and children, resentments among brothers and sisters, conflict on the job—all these painful experiences are intertwined and aggravated by our inability to deal well with our feelings . . . especially the feelings we have about ourselves.

How do you *feel* God *feels* about you?

Our feelings even affect our relationship with God. Occasionally, when I was pastoring I would take time during Sunday evening services to help people focus on their feelings. I might begin that part of the service by saying something like: "For the next few minutes, I would like for some of you to stand and tell us how you feel God feels about you."

Almost inevitably, the first person to speak would begin by saying, "I think God thinks..." Then, I would stop him and gently remind him of the instructions. He was to tell us how *he* felt God feels about *him*; not what *he* thought God thinks about *him.*

In spite of hearing what I had said to the previous person, the next person often would start out the same way, "Well, I think God thinks that..." So, I would have to stop *her*, too, and remind *her* that we were to focus on God's *feelings* toward us—not his *thoughts* about us!

God's feelings for us are on record!

The Scriptures are unmistakably clear in declaring how God feels about us.

> "You see, at just the right time, when we were still powerless, Christ died for the ungodly. Very rarely will anyone die for a righteous man, though for a good man someone might possibly dare to die. But God demonstrates his own love for us in this: While we were still sinners, Christ died for us. Since we have now been justified by his blood, how much more shall we be saved from God's wrath through him! For if, when we were God's enemies, we were reconciled to him through the death of his Son, how much more, having been reconciled, shall we be saved through his life!"[7]

When we begin to feel God's love poured into our hearts by the Holy Spirit and discover how deeply He loves us then we want to love Him in return. For some people, this becomes the first time in their lives they have felt truly loved by another person. Such a discovery of God's love often fills the aching void created by the absence of loving relationships with parents and siblings. At this point our relationship with God becomes based on His love for us and our love for Him. Only then is love likely to become the governing emotion in other relationships of our lives.

Problems between people begin within people.

It has been that way ever since Adam. Do you remember how he explained his disobedience to God? He blamed it all on Eve. When God confronted Eve, she was no more inclined to accept responsibility for her behavior than Adam was for his. She blamed it all on the serpent.[8]

However, where did their problems really begin? Adam's problems began within Adam . . . not Eve. Eve's problems began within Eve . . . not the serpent. Their problems were identical. Adam and Eve both chose to disobey God, but neither wanted to assume responsibility for their own disobedience.

Many of us choose to deny responsibility for our problems. It's too painful for us to face. Like Adam, we would rather make other people responsible for our troubles. And, we have an ingenious ability for doing this. If it is not convenient to blame our problems on others, we often blame them on the devil, like Eve did.

This is nothing new. As legend would have it, Martin Luther had a vision in which he saw the devil sitting by the side of the road crying. Luther approached the devil and asked him why he was crying. Satan said, "Because I get blamed for so many things I'm not responsible for!"

Problems between people usually begin as problems within people. If we were more skilled in identifying and managing problems within ourselves, we would have fewer problems with others.

Your self concept is the lens through which you see life.

Many of life's most painful problems flow out of our self concept. That was the message of a cartoon that showed a scrawny little fellow looking at himself in a mirror. The caption read, "Are you 'fer' me or 'ag'in' me today?" This is a very important question! Your best friend or worst enemy is the person you see when you look in the mirror.

The image we form of ourselves becomes the lens through which we look at life. After all, none of us sees life like it really is. We see it through the lens of our self-image. If your view of yourself is distorted your whole view of life will be twisted. Often I have discovered that the world looks amazingly different when I decide to clean the lenses of my own glasses rather than hand a bottle of lens cleaner to my family and friends. This is the moral of the following story.

"You'll find people like that wherever you go."

Before bridges were built, travelers were dependent on ferry boats to get them across the river. A wise old ferry boat captain made it a practice to talk to his passengers as he ferried them across the river.

One day, after picking up a load of passengers from one side he struck up a conversation with a woman who seemed to be terribly disturbed by her departure. Attempting to comfort her, he remarked, "I'm sorry to see you so upset?" She said, "I have never been so glad to get away from a place in all my life. People here are downright mean. They butter you up to your face, but behind your back they cut you up in little pieces and spit you out. I'm leaving some of the most hateful people I've ever known."

"Yes, Ma'am," agreed the old ferry boat captain. "You'll find people like that wherever you go."

Picking up a load of passengers from the other side of the river, he began to talk to another lady. Through her tears she said, "It breaks my heart to leave this place. I've never been around more loving people in my life. I've made wonderful friends here. I'm leaving a big piece of my heart in this place."

"Yes, Ma'am," the wise old ferry boat captain

chimed in. "You'll find people like that wherever you go."

As you can see, each of these ladies looked at life through her unique lens. Each made a very different impression on the old ferry boat captain. This was the result of the way each lady saw herself. He knew they would continue to see people the same way in the future as they had seen them in the past.

We can change the way we see others by changing the way we see ourselves. You were not born with the view you have of yourself. This is something you learned once you got here. Nor have you always felt about life the way you do today. Through the years, these feelings have grown out of the way you have learned to see yourself. The encouraging part about this is that anything we have learned we can modify and change.

What is a person's self-image?

Our self-image consists of those things we have chosen to believe to be true about ourselves. It is not formed from the way we see our self. It is formed from the way we feel other people see us. This does not mean other people actually see us this way. It only means this is the way we think they are viewing us. In other words, your self-image is not composed of who you think you are. It consists of who you think other people think you are.

To a great extent the way we see ourselves grows out of the way we believe our parents saw us when we were growing up. This is not necessarily the view our parents had of us, but it is the way we believe they viewed us. Once we started to school, the way we believed our teachers, peers and other significant adults viewed us also played an important role in further defining our self-image.

Sharpening the definition of your self-image

Your self-image consists of what you come to believe to be true about yourself. Unfortunately, if you were to ask many people, "What do you believe to be honest and true about yourself?" they couldn't tell you. They are so anxious and confused about life in general that their views of themselves are very uncertain and poorly defined.

A simple way to assess your self-image is to ask yourself, "How do I feel about the person I'm with when I'm alone?" You can learn a lot about how you feel and think about yourself by simply completing the following ten statements:

1. I am a person who_____.
2. I am a person who_____.
3. I am a person who_____.
4. I am a person who_____.
5. I am a person who_____.
6. I am a person who_____.
7. I am a person who_____.
8. I am a person who_____.
9. I am a person who_____.
10. I am a person who_____.

By filling in these blanks, you will discover ten things that you believe to be important and true about yourself. Why not do that now?

As you continue with the chapter you will notice how these statements color your view of yourself. They also affect the way you see God and the way you believe God sees you. In fact, it is difficult for you to have a healthy view of God without having a healthy view of yourself.

Here is the secret to being optimistic!

Our self-image is part of what Paul refers to as the

opaque glass through which we look at life.[9] Your view of
life is a product of your self-image. The more positively
you see yourself, the more optimistic your view of life will
be. The more negatively you see yourself, the more pessimistic your view of life will be.

Our fallen nature makes it impossible for us to see
life as God intended when He made us in His image. Sin
distorts our view. Our limited knowledge and experience
further warp our vision of reality. Your self-image either
adds clarity or confusion to this already distorted view of
your life. This is why it is so important.

How is your self-image formed?

None of us were born with preconceived ideas
about ourselves. Yet because memory is so highly corre-
lated with the acquisition of language we can't remember
a time when we didn't have definite feelings and ideas
about ourselves.

The two major components of our self-image are:
1. Our family and the environment in which we
were raised.
2. The way we chose to respond to our family and
that environment.

As you have learned, by the time we can talk we
already have a history of feelings that predisposes us to
positive or negative ways of seeing ourselves. Our use of
words only reinforces the ways we have already learned to
feel about ourselves. Words also give us the means of
expressing these feelings to others.

The view you have of yourself has grown out of
the complex interaction transpiring between you and your
family during the first three to five years of life. Your self-
image is affected by such things as the way your parents
felt about your arrival. After all, the arrival of a child is
not always planned or welcomed. It helps us when our

parents are pleased with our arrival...even if they didn't plan for it. The way parents feel about a baby's birth will be communicated to the child through subtle nuances of touch, sight, and sound during the times when they feed, bathe, and change the child.

There are also many other issues in those preverbal years that have an important bearing on your self-image: How often were you held and hugged? How gently or abruptly were you weaned? How patiently or impatiently were you toilet-trained? How did your parents react when they saw you fondle your genitals as an infant? How frequently were you yelled at and spanked? How often were you commended or criticized? How fairly or unfairly were you disciplined? How much freedom were you given? How much responsibility did they require of you?

How many times did your parents move before you started to school? What was the state of their marriage at the time? Did either of your parents lose close relatives to death during this time? Were any of your siblings seriously ill while you were this young?

None of these things should be viewed as determining your self-image. However, these, and many other experiences may have had an important bearing on the way you learned to feel about your self.

Although no child is born with a self-image, by the time we start to school, the ways we have learned to feel and think about ourselves are so obvious that any observant teacher readily recognizes them. Once formed, your self-image tends to be stable over time and highly resistant to change.

Birth order affects your self-image.

How many children were already in your family when you came along? How many came after you? Each person reacts to his or her birth order in a unique way, but some generalizations can be made about:

1. The first child

Some couples can hardly wait to have their first child. All their lives they have been looking forward to the opportunity to correct all the parenting mistakes they believe their parents made with them. So, the first child is the one many parents try to make perfect. Of course, we seldom do anything well the first time we attempt it and this includes parenting.

However, first children also have several advantages. They have both parents' full and undivided attention. Until their parents have another baby they do not have to share their parents' love and affection with other children. Nor do they have to share their toys. Parents give their first child more attention during those important early months than their other children will receive.

On the other hand, greater parental demands are made on the first child than on subsequent children. They are the oldest and are expected to know more than their brothers or sisters. Parents are often more demanding and critical of the first child. First children, however are also likely to receive more parental praise than later children.

Quite often, as a result of these unique factors, first children tend to be more conscientious and guilt prone. They are usually the family's first free babysitter. As adults they are often very responsible, highly productive people.   They tend to be "take charge" people and are frequently found in top levels of management.

2. The baby or an only child

Usually, older brothers and sisters are expected to make special allowances for the baby. So the baby often grows up expecting this from others in life. Of course, the longer it has been since the family has had a baby, the more family members will tend to cater to the baby.

Parents need to be sure that an "only child" has opportunities to learn social skills by mixing with other children their age. This allows them to learn the normal "give and take" one usually acquires from brothers and sisters. Such experiences help an "only child" learn to be less self-centered and more able to share with others.

Because of the love and attention they receive, only children are seldom insecure. However, like the baby of the family, they do tend to go through life expecting others to give in to them and take care of them.

Parents who have only one child may find it difficult to allow the normal risk-taking behavior that teaches a child confidence in his or her ability to survive. This kind of an over-protective parent may produce a dependent, insecure child.

3. The middle child

The middle child holds the "good news" - "bad news" position in the family. They lack the attention given to the first child and the baby of the family. When there are only three children, the middle child has an enviable opportunity to compete with his or her siblings for parental love and attention. This gives the middle child a chance to master a skill that our society rewards handsomely—competition.

However, in a large family, middle children are most likely to suffer from negative self-images. They are not close enough to the front or back of the line to get the love and nurturance they need to feel good about who they are. Often, therefore, they grow up more prone to be anxious and depressed than their brothers and sisters.

How much love and affection was in your home?

The amount of love and affection in your home

makes an important difference in your self concept. This is why our staff asks any adult reaching out to us for help, "As a child, how did you know your parents loved each other?"

An adult with fond memories of family affection is more likely to have a positive self-image than one raised in a family lacking affection. So, I'm always glad to get the kind of response that one man who was raised in the south gave me. He said, "I knew my Momma and Daddy loved each other because of the way they were always a lovin' on one another." Children brought up in homes with plenty of affection are to be envied.

Usually, when we ask people that question, there is a long pause as they begin to reflect. Finally, we are likely to hear, "Well, there wasn't much affection in our home. I seldom heard my parents say they loved each other. So, I guess I just took that for granted because they stayed together."

Another important question

How did you know your parents loved you? People with the most scarred and distorted images of themselves have a difficult time recalling how they knew their dad and mom loved them. They were seldom held, hugged or kissed. They were seldom told they were loved.

If you remember having healthy feelings about yourself as a child, thank God for your parents. And if your parents are alive, call them and write to them often to thank them for the good start they gave you in life.

Birth order and the amount of affection in your family are just two of many variables that make up the matrix from which your self-image comes. More important than these factors, however, is how you chose to react to them.

Exert your control where it counts.

We have little or no control over the choices our parents or others made in determining our environment. However, we do have control over how we choose to respond to that environment.

Over the years, I have seen people from very similar environments turn out very different in life. Some raised in supportive environments have chosen to see themselves in a very negative way. Others have grown up in horribly destructive environments and managed to preserve a very positive self-image.

When we are growing up, many events of our lives are beyond our control. As adults we do not live with those events, we live a memory of them that is filtered through our self-image.

Your self-image is your key to happiness.

Your happiness is largely determined by how you feel and think about yourself—and how you choose to feel and think about what has happened to you in life. Remember our self-image becomes the lens through which we look at life. Solomon said it well: "As he thinks in his heart, so is he."[10]

Jesus expanded on this important truth, "Out of the overflow of the heart the mouth speaks. The good man brings good things out of the good stored up in him, and the evil man brings evil things out of the evil stored up in him."[11]

What do these verses mean? Jesus is simply explaining that you can know much about the content of a person's heart from listening to his or her conversation. This is also a basic tenet of psychology.

When you listen to people talk, they tell you what is in their heart. A person is unable to keep quiet about what he has an abundance of in his heart. Whatever the heart is full of inevitably will surface in conversation.

Listen to what you say when you talk to others. What are your favorite topics of conversation? How broadly conversant are you with the issues of the day? Is there depth to your conversation or do you major in trivia? When you talk about people, do you generally tend to build them up or do you tear them down? As you analyze your philosophy of life from your conversation, is it optimistic or pessimistic?

How do you talk to yourself?

As important as your conversation with others may be, the way you talk to yourself is even more important. After all, what you say to other people is just a sample of what you keep telling yourself. The way you talk to yourself grows out of and contributes to your self-image.

For example, if you have grown up with the idea that other people are smarter than you are, emotionally healthier than you are, and more likable than you are, then you are going to feel inferior and insecure much of the time. And as long as you express this view to yourself it will be reflected in your conversations with others.

When I have tried to assure people that they can see life much more positively, they have told me, "You just don't know what it was like in my family when I was growing up." I usually respond with, "What happens to us in life is not nearly as important as the way we choose to respond to it. After all, none of us lives with just the events of his or her life. We live with a story we tell ourselves about these events."

Our memories are comprised of these stories. Neither the events nor the facts which describe them can be changed, but our memories can be edited. Isn't this a redemptive thought?

None of us grows up in ideal circumstances. One of life's big deceptions is that if we had another person's circumstances we would be happier. However, even if we had someone else's circumstances, we would still interpret them in our own way. This becomes obvious in the following story.

"He can't swim, can he?"

A duck hunter invested a sizeable sum of money in a great retriever. The first time this hunter took his dog hunting, no one else was with him. On his first shot, a duck fell into the water. Immediately, the dog walked out on the water, picked up the game in his mouth, and returned it to his master. This dog was something else! The man couldn't believe his own eyes. The same thing happened three more times before the day was over; so, the hunter was elated.

As he stowed his game and gear in his van, he thought to himself, "I could never tell anybody about what I saw today. No one would believe me. Everyone will think I am crazy." So he decided he would take a hunting buddy with him the next time he went duck hunting. He did.

The day went just like it had gone when he was alone. Every time he or his buddy would shoot a duck, the dog would walk out on the water, pick it up, and bring it back to them. The friend gave no indication that he noticed anything different about the dog.

Finally, while they were packing their game and gear back into the van, the dog's proud owner couldn't stand his friend's silence any longer. So, he turned to his friend and asked, "Did you notice anything unusual about my dog today?" "Yeah," his friend replied, "He can't swim, can he?"

The point I am making is that you view your own

experiences and those of others in your own way. Regard-less of how unusual or even miraculous they may be you see them from your own perspective. Circumstances don't determine your happiness. It is the way you chose to view them and talk to yourself about them that becomes critical to your happiness.

A person with a negative self-image can be in the most positive circumstances and not find anything to be encouraged about. On the other hand, a person with a pos-itive self-image can weather some very severe storms in life and not be done in by them. The way you see it is the way it is for you!

Everyone's skies have their dark clouds.

People who don't know me have often said to me, "You can say all that about interpreting your circum-stances positively, because life has been kinder to you than it has to me." I suppose it's easy for us to assume that life has treated other people better than it has treated us, espe-cially if we don't know them.

What follows is such a central part of my life I want to share it with you even though a similar account appears in another book of mine.

My mother was married the first time when she was 15. Her husband brutalized her, so she divorced him. When she was 18, she married my father. When she was 19, they were expecting me. Thirteen days after my birth, she died. My birth killed my mother.

My aunt had been married and was left a widow with a little girl. So, when my father needed somebody to take care of me and she needed help in taking care of her little girl, the two of them got married. My cousin became my step-sister.

Then, six years later, my dad and my aunt had a girl of their own. So, I grew up in a home where it was,

"Your kid, my kid, and our kid." We had a "blended fami-ly" before sociologists taught us what to call it.

Much later in my life I married, and my first wife died of cancer. We had been married for 47 years. She was a very godly woman who had enjoyed unusually good health all of her life. Although we had never talked about it, both of us assumed she would outlive me. I'm sure the children did as well.

The nagging pain she felt in her lower back was the first indication we had that she was ill. Four months later, through a series of diagnostic tests, the doctors gave us the shocking news. She had non-Hodgkins lymphoma. They assured us that the chances of her beating the illness were good.

In the meantime, well-intentioned people would assure us she would be healed. We fasted and prayed. Hundreds of others prayed as well. Yet, in spite of all this and the best of medical care, I watched her lose battle after battle for her life.

Chemotherapy and radiation gave us some quality time, but during the last six months the children and I saw her slipping away from us. We kept her at home which is what she wanted. We watched her lose touch with us and leave for Heaven in June 1992.

This is just a little peek into the pages of my life, but I hope it helps you see that pain and trouble come to everyone. No one's skies are sunny all the time! We all have our storms. The way we talk to ourselves about these storms determines how sunny or dark the skies of our lives will be.

Remember, our inner speech involves not only the facts of our history, but also encases the emotional impact those events have had on us.

You talk to yourself at amazing speeds.

When you talk to yourself you speak a different form of your language than you do when talking to others. This is what enables you to speak to yourself so much faster than you can talk to others or they can talk to you.

Your inner speech is not burdened with the formalities demanded when you are speaking with others. It is "characterized by four interdependent attributes" that enable you to rapidly mediate very complex urges, fantasies and ideas. First, inner speech is silent. Second, unlike public speech which must fully represent what you are trying to say, inner speech is syntactically crushed. Third, in talking to yourself you use elliptical words which represent the mere skin of a thought loaded with multiple complex associations and rich emotional content you don't have to articulate when speaking to yourself. Fourth, since inner speech is private it does not have to make sense to anyone else but you.

Korba timed people in solving simple problems and then asked them to put in writing the inner speech involved in reaching their conclusions. When they did this, "the extended word count represented an equivalent rate of speech in excess of 4,000 words per minute."[12]

A simple example of this kind of compressed inner speech might be found in imagining yourself at a baseball game when all of a sudden a line drive is zooming its way toward your head. Are you going to say to yourself, "Wow! There is a baseball approaching my head at an unbelievable speed. I must duck before I am seriously injured?" Probably not. In a fraction of a second your inner speech is more likely to be something like, "Ball ... duck!" However, when you tell your friends who were not with you what happened you will have to use many more words in describing that lightning-like conversation you had with yourself in order to escape injury.

This speed of your mental activity is what makes it is so easy for your thoughts to stray when you are bored by what others are saying to you. In those moments, your mind conveniently provides you a welcome escape by opening up to you more interesting side trips into your yesterdays or tomorrows.

Others who try to help you change the way you feel and think about the events of your life, can only talk to you at the rate of two to three hundred words per minute. Basically, this is what limits their efforts to "make you happy."

Only you can change your feelings

God knows that your happiness is too important for Him to put in anyone's hands but yours—and His. It is unfair for any of us to expect someone else to change the way we feel about ourselves or the way we feel about life. Nor do I want anyone else determining whether I'm going to be happy. I want that freedom and responsibility for myself.

If in the process of growing up in your home, you were given a wholesome self-image; then this is one part of your life that doesn't need to change. However, many of us were born to parents who were preoccupied with their own pain at the time we came into their lives. They were unaware of how we were learning to feel and think about ourselves as we interacted with them.

They wouldn't have intentionally given us a miserable way of looking at life, or a negative way of seeing ourselves, but hurts from their past and pressures from their present blinded them to how we were learning to view life. Concern for our emotional comfort was lost in their efforts to survive their own pain.

Regeneration makes recreation possible.

Can a person who has a damaged self-image change the way he feels and thinks about himself? Yes, thank God, he can. This is one of the great blessings of being born again.

Paul tells us that we can be changed gradually into the image of Christ.[13] Just as your natural self-image grew out of your relationship with your earthly parents you can discover and develop a new way of looking at yourself out of your interaction with your heavenly Father.

Once we are born again, we have the opportunity of becoming the person God knows we can be in Jesus. What we do with this opportunity is left to our own choices.

For many of us, achieving this goal requires the transformation of a badly damaged self-image we brought with us into God's kingdom. The directions of God's Word and the dynamics of His Spirit are divine resources at our disposal in pursuit of this goal. However, if we are going to be changed we have to take the initiative in applying these resources to the continual conversations we are having with ourselves about the circumstances and events of our lives.

How can we go about changing our self-image?

Many believers seem to expect this to happen magically at the instant of conversion, with little or no personal involvement. Although the miracle of God's grace is an essential dynamic in any such transformation, it also requires us to put forth a conscious and deliberate effort in the process.

God doesn't expect you to do what you can't, but He does expect you to do what you can. Here are some practical steps you can take toward a wholesome self-image.

1. See yourself as a person God loves very much.

Certainly there is nothing about the fallen nature of the human race that makes us lovable. Even a casual look at our collective history reveals us to be self-destructive and detestable. And our personal history justifies the same conclusion. However, through His grace, God has chosen to love us. He wants us to see ourselves as children who are loved dearly by their Heavenly Father.

This will be a new way for some to see themselves. The lack of love and affirmation in the history of many Christians makes it difficult for them to believe that they are dearly loved by God. Some see themselves in such a negative way as to make receiving a simple compliment difficult for them. How easy is it for you to accept a compliment? When someone says, "Oh, you look so nice tonight," do you find it necessary to tell him or her you bought your dress on sale or got your suit at a discount? Are you likely to respond to a compliment with an apology? Is it difficult for you to simply say, "Thank you, I appreciate that"?

How easy is it for you to receive expressions of love from others? Can you see why they would love you? Do you see yourself as someone God loves very much? He wants you to see yourself this way.

Regardless of how you may feel your earthly parents viewed you, when you look at the Cross, there should never be any doubt about your heavenly Father's feelings about you. Remember, Calvary does not tell you how much God loves you as His child. Calvary only tells you how much God loved you when you were His enemy.

If you want to remember how much God loves you as His child, I would suggest that you make a cross somewhere in the front of your Bible. Above that cross write the question, "How much does God love me?" In answering this question simply write over the cross the words, "God loves me much more!"[14]

Can you fathom that? God loves you and me more than Calvary can express. This is the way your heavenly Father wants you to see yourself.

2. Realize you are very valuable to God.

.   One of the common afflictions I see believers suffering from is very low self-worth. They simply do not understand the difference between being unworthy and being worthless. They make a mental equation of the two words. To them, being unworthy is the same as being worthless.

As we mentioned earlier these terms are not synonymous. Being unworthy is not the same as being worthless. None of us can ever be worthy of the price our heavenly Father paid for us. How could we ever be proud enough to think that we were worthy of Calvary? However, God imputed that worth to us.

You may be thinking of the Scripture that says when we've done everything we ought to do, we should consider ourselves unprofitable servants.[15] That's true – we are unprofitable, but not worthless.

Remember that profit is an economic term. It refers to the amount returned to the investor in excess of the amount of his expenses. How can you and I return to God an amount in excess of the price He paid for our redemption? That is impossible! If I were to do everything I could to repay my heavenly Father for the price of my redemption, I still would have to consider myself very unprofitable.

Jesus did not tell that parable to make us feel worthless. He simply wants us to know that Calvary was no business deal for our heavenly Father. It was a love affair! And love never looks for profit.

Your heavenly Father loves you very much. He also considers you extremely valuable to Him. So, begin to say over and over again in your mind, "God loves me very much. I am very valuable to Him."

3. Think of yourself as a forgiven person.

Many people suffer the needless pain of unhealthy guilt. They unconsciously assume there is some virtue in continuing to suffer for their own sins. But the truth is that Christ's sufferings atoned for our sins. And when He suffered, He not only suffered enough for my sins and yours, He suffered enough for the sins of the whole world.[16] So there is no virtue to be gained in our continuing to punish ourselves for our own sins. Jesus suffered enough for all of us.

You may have to live with the natural consequences of some poor choices that you made, but it is never God's will for you to continue to suffer guilt for sins from which Jesus has cleansed you. For example, a person may drive his automobile under the influence of alcohol and lose a limb in an accident. He will never regain his limb, but God doesn't want him to suffer additional crippling guilt the rest of his life because he drove when he was drunk.

There is no sin you can confess that God won't forgive. Satan, as your accuser, may put self-condemning thoughts into your mind.[17] He may suggest that what you did at some point in your past is too wicked for even God to forgive. But remember, he's a liar.[18] God's Word reassures us that if we confess our sins God is faithful to forgive them.

If you have confessed your sin to Christ, He has forgiven it.[19] So, practice saying to yourself, "I am a forgiven person." Say that to yourself over and over again until every bit of guilt from your past is gone - under the blood of Christ - never to be remembered against you again.

4. See yourself as a person who can change.

At times the process of change may require us to

"pray through" some of our old hurts. I have discovered this form of creative prayer to be very effective in my own life and have used it in helping many others.

Creative prayer is simply asking God to provide something for you or others that is not obvious to you or them at the moment. It is a form of petitionary prayer.

"Praying through" is a specific kind of creative prayer that enables you to discover healing and redemptive ways of looking at the destructive parts of your past. The enemy's version of your past is much more destructive than is warranted by the circumstances. Jesus has a creative way for you to see whatever is back there.

In "praying through" God will help you edit painful parts of your past. Since praying through often involves expressing intense feelings to God, I encourage people to do this when they are alone. Here are the four steps in the process of "praying through":

A. Talk to God honestly about what hurts you.

Great men and women of Scripture have always found the courage to be honest with God, and so can you. It isn't easy, but it is the only way prayer can bring you the practical help you need when life is hurting you.

This is the way Jacob resolved the issues of guilt and fear he suffered over his dealings with Esau. He spent a painful night in prayer coming to terms with those feelings.[20] Read about David's honesty in baring his heart to God over his affair with Bathsheba.[21] And, don't forget the bitter tears Peter shed over his denial of Christ.[22] Determine to talk to God honestly about the issues in your life that are keeping you from seeing yourself the way God sees you in Christ.

B. Express your feelings about your hurts to God.

As you begin to talk to God honestly about your

hurts the feelings associated with those hurts will surface. You may want to weep. You may find yourself expressing intensely angry feelings to God. David did. He begs God to break the teeth of his enemies. In another place he prays, "For the sins of their mouths, for the words of their lips, let them be caught in their pride. For the curses and lies they utter, consume them in wrath, consume them till they are no more. Then it will be known to the ends of the earth that God rules over Jacob. They return at evening, snarling like dogs and prowl about the city. They wander about for food and howl if not satisfied."[23]

You may be thinking, "But I don't want God to know I feel that way about my enemies." Now, think how ridiculous that is!

If those feelings are there, how can you hide them from God? You need to get those feelings out in the presence of someone who will keep them confidential and someone you can trust with them. Even though you would never act out those feelings, burying them inside of you can keep you from enjoying life. You need to express them to God.

As you pour your feelings out to God in a time of private prayer, you will reach a time when you have emptied your soul. Everything bottled up inside you has been poured out before the Lord. The burden of your heart has lifted. You are now ready for step three.

C. Meditate on a new meaning for your old hurts.

You can never think differently about your old hurts until you feel differently about them. Remember what we said earlier: you experience life through your feelings and your thoughts. However, once you've emptied out your old feelings before God, you are in a position for Him to comfort you and show you a new way of feeling and thinking about them.

Just as God helped David turn loose of his hatred and bitterness toward those who had hurt him, the Lord will help you surrender your hurts and will suggest new and more constructive ways of looking at them as you quietly meditate before Him.

Remember David's prayer, "Search me, O God, know my heart: test me and know my anxious thoughts. See if there is any offensive way in me, and lead me in the way everlasting."[24]

D. Praise God for the new meaning He gives you!

As God helps you to see your old hurts in a new and less painful way, thank Him and praise Him. Repeat the new meaning several times in praise and prayer. That way when Satan brings the old meaning to your mind again you will have learned and embedded the new one so deeply that the old one has no more grip on you.

Don't expect all of this to happen in just one session of creative prayer. It may require several sessions to bring the needed relief and healing. After all, we didn't get the way we are in minutes, and we're not likely to become completely different in just minutes. "Praying through" is a lot like peeling an onion. The pain disappears a layer at a time and you may cry a lot.

The change you seek is much more likely to result from this kind of a disciplined process of prayer. But that process has to start sometime in your life, so, why not let it start now?

First, remind yourself that no one comes into this world with any preconceived ideas about himself or herself.

Second, remember that you learned the way you feel and think about yourself during the third through fifth years of your life. Asking other family members to tell you what was happening in your home during these years may shed some useful insight on why you reached such distorted and painful conclusions about yourself. Often, small children blame themselves for family tragedies and live many years with the sad consequences of such mistaken ideas.

Third, realize that anything you have learned you can unlearn and replace with new learning. These are the goals of praying through.

Fourth, remember God does not want you to live in the shadow of your past. So, determine that you will not let the consequences of any poor decisions you may have made earlier in your life deprive you of the peace and joy Jesus came to bring you. Saul of Tarsus persecuted and killed Christians. His memory of those past horrors could have haunted him for the rest of his life, but he determined to forget his past. And so can you!

It doesn't make any difference how old you are. Your future can be different and better than your past. God doesn't want you to be crippled by the pain of your past. He has more wholesome ways for you to view whatever may be there.

God not only wants to heal you from your past, He wants you to be able to see yourself as He sees you: someone he loves, values, forgives, and changes.

The next time you look in a mirror, I want you to say, "I'm looking at someone God loves very much. I'm looking at someone God says is very valuable to Him. I'm looking at someone who has been totally forgiven. I'm looking at someone who is changing and becoming more like Jesus."

When we begin to see ourselves in Jesus then the world will begin to see Jesus in us. Then, we are well on our way to defeating our self-consciousness and fears. In our next chapter, we will be taking a closer look at these would-be giants who threaten to keep us from our

Promised Land. We will also find some practical ways of dealing with them.

Discussion Questions

1. According to 1 Corinthians 6:19, 20 and 1 Peter 1:18, 19 what ultimately establishes our worth?
2. Where do your feelings about yourself come from?
3. How do parents affect a child's self-image?
4. What role do we play in the formation of our own self-images?
5. What is the dark glass through which we look at life (1 Corinthians 13:12) and how does it become distorted?
6. How does God feel about His enemies? His children?
7. Why is your self-image so important? Give examples.
8. When a person has a destructive history, how can he or she have a healthy self-image without denying the facts?
9. Discuss "praying through" and its affect on a person's self-image.
10. Why is talking to God "honestly" about our hurts so difficult?

FOOTNOTES

[1]Proverbs 21:4
[2]Mark 8:36-37
[3]"The reconciliation of God and man through the sacrificial death of Jesus Christ," *Merriam-Webster Collegiate Dictionary, 2000, ver 2.5*
[4]1 Peter 1:18-19; Romans 8:32
[5]Genesis 1:27
[6]Brody, Leslie R., and Hall, Judith A., **Gender and Emotion**, in *Handbook of Emotion, eds. Michael Lewis and Jeanette Havilland*, New York: Guilford Press, 1993, p.454.
[7]Romans 5:6-10
[8]Genesis 3:13
[9]1 Corinthians 13:12
[10]Proverbs 23:7
[11]Matthew 12:34-35
[12]Korba, Rodney. "The Rate of Inner Speech," **Perceptual and Motor Skills, 1990, 71, 1044.**
[13]2 Corinthians 3:18
[14]Romans 5:9
[15]Luke 17:10
[16]1 John 2:2
[17]Revelation 12:10
[18]John 8:44
[19]1 John 1:9
[20]Genesis 32:13-32
[21]Psalms 51:1-19
[22]Luke 22:62
[23]Psalms 59:12-15
[24]Psalms 129:33

CHAPTER FOUR

NOTHING TO FEAR
BUT FEAR
ITSELF

It was the Great Depression. America was in the paralyzing grip of financial disaster. A record number of banks were being forced to close. The institutions of our country were in disarray.

Almost overnight panic on Wall Street had wiped out the family fortunes of Americans. People had gone to bed as millionaires and gotten up the next day as paupers. The tragedy of their losses drove many to suicide.

Thousands of people had their homes repossessed by the banks. Before it was over my grandparents had lost three homes. More than 13 million were unemployed. Only breadlines stood between millions of Americans and starvation. The country was on the brink of anarchy and revolution.

Franklin Delano Roosevelt, former governor of the state of New York, had just been elected president of the United States. In his first inaugural address he rose to the challenge of this dismal occasion by inspiring courage in the American people through his famous declaration, "So, first of all, let me assert my firm belief that the only thing we have to fear is fear itself—nameless, unreasoning, unspecified terror which paralyzes needed efforts to convert retreat into advance."[1]

The president knew fear's destructive power was the nation's greatest enemy and, from his own personal battle with polio, he had discovered the creative power of hope and courage. So, he challenged the American people to advance beyond their fears—and they did!

Everyone knows what it is to be afraid.

Fear and anxiety are more of a problem for some than for others. But, no human being lives totally free from fear. This crippling emotion is as old as the human race. It was the consequence of Adam's fall.[2]

Once we are born, fear's shadow is never far away. But, before we are born we have an environment free from fear. Nestled in the womb, we are comforted by the sound of our mother's heartbeat. Life is never more comfortable or secure for us than during those last few weeks inside our mother.

Birth introduces us to fear.

The birth experience involves a strange downward movement of falling which is startling and frightening for us. Without warning we find ourselves thrust into the world outside our mother! No longer does she supply our oxygen, we must learn to get it from the air. We must breathe on our own. Our food is no longer served automatically. We must also find that for ourselves. So, we experience hunger for the first time in our lives. Our automatic waste disposal is discontinued. Now, others seem to have great concern about when, where, and how we eliminate. And for the first time, we are introduced to a diaper!

Evidence of this introduction to fear is found in the startle reflex obvious when you hold a baby in your arms and lower them rapidly. The mother's body has always been there to provide support for the baby. This rapid loss of support spreads a look of terror across the baby's face.

Some adults find it amusing to see the baby extending their arms and legs in this kind of a panicky startle response. But, this experience is very frightening for a baby and should never be indulged in as a form of adult entertainment.

This fear of falling is so deeply rooted in our

unconscious memory that we may dream about falling from time to time. How many times have you awakened at night by a dream of falling? This feeling is so real and frightening that jerking to avoid it is what wakes us up.

Babies fear abandonment.

When birth is viewed through the baby's eyes one can begin to understand the newborn's fear of abandonment. Several weeks before birth, the fetus is surrounded by a world of mother's sounds—her body fluids and, most important, her heartbeat. These are a familiar part of the unborn child's world and a reminder of mother's continual presence.

Birth drastically changes the baby's environment and the nature of the relationship between the mother and her baby. Before birth, the baby is engulfed in a totally caring environment. The birth process forces the fetus out of mother's body so the baby is no longer close enough to hear mother's familiar body fluids and reassuring heartbeat. For the first time in the baby's short history, there is no physical attachment to mother. At times, she is no longer there. As adults we have a difficult time realizing how abandoned newborns must feel in a moment like that and how frightening it must be for them.

Newborns live in a world of *total experience!*

What is a world of total experience? It is an unmediated world. You and I mediate our world through the words we use to describe it to ourselves. If we use our words in a healthy way they enable us to lessen our pains and increase our pleasures. However, until babies can talk they have no way of mediating their life experiences.

So, theirs is a world of total pain or total pleasure. When the baby's skin is caught in its diaper the baby is unable to say, "Wow, does this hurt. If mother knew my diaper was pinching me like this she would take my diaper off and put it on again somewhat looser so that it wouldn't pinch me."

All the baby knows is that he or she is in pain. There is no way for the child to mediate that pain. The baby does not know the pain is unintentional or that it will be temporary. From the baby's perspective it is likely to last forever. The baby is in total pain!

But, when the baby has a full stream of warm milk coming from mother's breast or a bottle, the baby has no way of realizing the pleasure will not last forever. Then, the baby is in a world of total pleasure!

During these months of total experience it is important that the baby experience more pleasure than pain. A totally pain-free life is not a realistic hope, but if there is more pain than pleasure the baby learns that this world is a painful place. However, when the baby experiences more pleasure than pain, he or she is likely to interpret life experiences in a much more positive way.

The fear of falling, the fear of pain, and the fear of abandonment are the three great fears in an infant's world. These begin our long history with fear and none is exempt from it.

Childhood fears

When we are small our fears are mostly related to our physical survival. Do you remember your early childhood fears? I do. I can remember lying on my bed at night watching the shadow of tree limbs swaying in the wind. Until I was old enough to know what I was seeing, I would imagine those shadows were all kinds of ghosts coming after me.

Most parents have to help their small children through such painful irrational fears. Often these fears surface at night. The wise parent will keep a light on in the child's bedroom to dispel the shadows. Even this may not be enough to provide the comfort a child needs.

For a few nights, it may be necessary for a parent to stay in the child's bedroom with him until he goes to sleep. The light plus the reassuring presence of mom or dad should help the child conquer his fear. However, soon the light alone will be all the child needs. Finally, he will develop the courage to turn the light off and go to sleep in the dark.

Fear of the dark, fear of snakes, fear of spiders— these are only a few of the many specific fears of children. Through our parents' love we usually grow out of our specific fears by the time we are eight or nine.

Fear is tormenting![3]

I vividly recall the tormenting fear that gripped me in the middle of the night many years ago. My first wife and I were spending the night with my parents. When my mother got up to go to the bathroom she looked out of the bedroom window and noticed a man bent over the trunk of our car parked in my parents' driveway. She came into our bedroom, awakened us and said, "Son, I think someone is trying to steal your car."

When we went to the window we saw a man bending down and looking at the trunk of our car. From what we saw we concluded that he was preparing to break into the trunk.

I was so frightened that when I called the police to report what was going on I couldn't talk out loud. So, I began to whisper to them over the phone. Finally, the man who was taking the information assured me that if I would keep the lights off in the house it was perfectly safe for me to talk loud enough to be heard over the phone.

You can understand how foolish we all felt when we discovered that we had called the police to apprehend

my grandparents who had tried to surprise us by coming
back from Florida a day early. My grandfather was the
man we had seen leaning over to inspect the license plate
of my car. He was trying to figure out whose car it was.
Because they didn't recognize my car they thought my
parents had overnight guests. So, not wanting to intrude
they decided to spend the rest of the night in their car. By
the time the police arrived on the scene my grandparents
were sound asleep. I can't imagine how startled they must
have been when they were abruptly awakened by the glare
of the policeman's flashlight shining in their faces.

The officer came to the door and said, "I'm sure
you don't want us to arrest these people. They are your
parents and grandparents." After the family recovered
from this kind of frightening reunion, we all enjoyed a
hearty laugh.

This is the degree to which fear can blur our judgment and render us powerless. When we are afraid we
cannot think clearly or act wisely. Is it any wonder that
Jesus repeatedly encouraged His disciples not to be
afraid?[4] He knows that fear keeps us from seeing creative
options in problem-solving and decision-making that He
wants to show us.

Fear also tends to paralyze and blind.

Some time ago I sat with a pregnant teenager.
She and the teenage father had met at church. She was a
believer, but he wasn't. They had gone together for several months. He had convinced her that he loved her dearly
and wanted to marry her. He said they were just as good
as married in God's sight. When she told him she was
pregnant, however, he angrily rejected her and wouldn't
even talk to her over the phone.

By the time she talked to me she had already seen
her pastor who had helped her confess her sin to the Lord.

She had found the forgiveness she needed. God gave her the courage to resist the pressure her boyfriend and his family had put on her to have an abortion.

Now she was struggling with the remaining options. None of them were good. Should she allow the baby to be adopted through a Christian child placement agency? Should she keep the baby and raise him or her by herself? Would any other man want to marry her if she insisted on bringing this child into their marriage? Should she marry the child's father?

What are the chances that a teenager can overcome the fear and anxiety of such a moment sufficiently to consider wisely the complexity of questions like these? It is extremely difficult for anyone, regardless of their age, to see the best option in such a pressure-packed situation.

Christians are never alone in their fears.

Even though people's poor choices put them in this kind of a painful situation, they don't need to add to their pain by assuming God has forsaken them. He hasn't. And He won't.

So I assured this teenager, "If you will open your mind and spirit to God, He will help you discern which of these remaining options is best for you and for your baby. You can trust Him to guide you."

After thoroughly discussing each of these options I had prayed with her. I asked God to help her overcome her fear, rise above the pressure of the moment and deny the insistence of her own desires so that she could see the option He would persistently bring to her mind.

As she left my office, she thanked me for making her aware of the ways her fear and anxiety could blind and cripple her. She assured me that she was determined to find and do God's will.

Later, I learned that a Christian adoption agency

had found a home for her baby. Several years later I met this baby and the couple who adopted him. They were pastors of a large church who were kind enough to have me as a pulpit guest. They gave the boy a wonderful home. They were delighted that I was able to acquaint them with the circumstances of the boy's conception and provide them information about his parents.

This young mother learned to trust God for wisdom in a frightening moment in her life. Later in her life she met a man who loved God, loved her and married her. Just as God was there for her He will be there for you.

Let's take a look at some ways of telling the difference between healthy and unhealthy fears. Then we'll take a look at some effective means of defeating fear—ways that utilize Scripture and are consistent with your faith.

Many crippling fears are irrational.

Through the years I have seen many men and women whose lives have been paralyzed by fears that were not obvious to others or easily understood by them. For example, some people are so fearful of germs and disease that they are gripped by an overwhelming compulsion to wash their hands dozens or more times a day. Of course I'm not talking about the normal need for cleanliness or even scrupulous sanitation.

Compulsive hand washing indicates a fear of germs (misophobia) that goes far beyond the most scrupulous actions of a person who is simply cautious about personal cleanliness. A person who suffers from misophobia may wash his or her hands as often as a hundred times a day. Other people are so fearful of social situations they cannot leave their homes by themselves. They are literally prisoners in their own homes. People crippled by this illness (agoraphobia) cannot be employed unless their work is in their home.

Regardless of how ridiculous such fears may seem to others, they are very real to the sufferer. Without competent professional help, these people are likely to remain victims of their fears for years, if not for life. Even with professional help, recovery may be slow and difficult. This is why it is so important to see unhealthy fears and recognize them as a devastating enemy early in life when they are much more easily defeated. Remember, unhealthy fears almost always can be conquered once they are identified.

Healthy vs. unhealthy fear

What is the difference between healthy and unhealthy fear? Healthy fears protect us from dangerous places, practices and people.

All fear is painful, but the pain of healthy fears is our friend. It warns us of danger. If I cut my foot I could bleed to death if my foot didn't cause me enough pain to bring the wound to my attention.

Because the brain associates pain and pleasure with places and persons, children can experience healthy fears without the risk of being hurt. They don't have to burn themselves on things that are hot in order to know that hot things can hurt them. They can learn the dangers of playing in open stairwells without falling down the stairs. They can learn that sharp things can cut and must be handled with care without being wounded. Without the pain of healthy fears we couldn't learn these important lessons of survival.

Healthy emotional fears empower our conscience. They protect our relationships with God and the significant people in our lives. Healthy fears warn us of the painful consequences of disobedience.

By inflicting appropriate emotional pain on us our parents dealt with our disobedience. I don't feel I was abused, but at times, I was "reared." In my memories I can still feel it. Healthy fear of the consequences of disobedience taught me to keep my behavior in bounds.

Healthy fear teaches people healthy limits.   It helps us to be law abiding citizens. It makes our behavior predictable and orderly. Without this, society would not be possible. These are all healthy fears.

The most important of our healthy fears is fear of the Lord. Solomon says this is the beginning of wisdom.[5] The fear of the Lord is not terrifying it is an awesome reverence born when we experience the presence of God. Unfortunately, many people confuse being afraid of God with the fear of the Lord. Persons with a healthy faith are not afraid of God. If you are afraid of God you have had to learn that fear. Awe and reverence of Him are healthy, but God does not want His children to be afraid of Him.

You learn "the fear of the Lord" when you first experience His presence. For some people this happens in nature. Others discover Him at church. Regardless of where you first encounter God, it leaves an indelible impression on you. You never forget it. A reverence for God is forged in your mind and you carry this overwhelming sense of awe and wonder throughout life.

What makes such an encounter with God the beginning of wisdom for us? Becoming aware of His presence establishes our ultimate accountability and makes us aware of our responsibility for the choices we make in life. This sense of responsibility helps us order the priorities of our lives more wisely. It puts a different perspective on life. Material concerns become less important to us than spiritual ones. His awesome presence helps us make wiser choices in life. It gives us a more accurate way of counting the cost of sensual pleasure.

Unhealthy fears

Many people are dominated by religious terror. It's not awe. It's not wonder. It's not reverence. It's terror! This is the most crippling of our unhealthy fears. People held in this kind of religious terror see God suspending them over hell by a thread. They fear the return of Christ. They fear the "mark of the beast."[6] They fear death. Some even fear they have committed some unpardonable sin.[7]

You may have felt that way. Please know that the Holy Spirit never put such a thought in your mind. That thought was probably sown by some over-zealous, but misinformed teacher, preacher, or parent.

You can take comfort in the fact that among the hundreds of people I have seen for counseling, I have never met one whose sins were unpardonable. God never wills for people to suffer the terror of thinking they have committed "the unpardonable sin." Because this problem is the source of so much torment for so many people, I will deal with it in detail in Chapter 5.

Self-consciousness is a form of fear.

Often, people miss many opportunities in life because of self-consciousness. No one is born self-conscious. This is something the small child acquires over a period of time.

What is self-consciousness? It is the feeling of being observed, but not approved. The sensitive child is more prone to be self-conscious, but any child who discovers the approval of his or her parental figures difficult to obtain is at risk for being crippled by this fear of rejection.

Self-consciousness can mentally paralyze you. For example, regardless of a speaker's experience, if people in the audience begin to act uninterested or look at him in disapproving ways, it will be very difficult for him to think clearly and to express himself well.

Paul addresses this possibility in his letter to Timothy. He did not want him to be intimidated by the enemies of the Gospel. So, he reminds Timothy that his faith is the product of three generations.[8] He assures him that God had not given him a spirit of timidity, but of power, of love, and of self-discipline.[9]

The Greek word "deilia" translated "fear" can be more accurately understood to mean "timidity." Paul's reference to a "sound mind" in the King James Version has nothing to do with Timothy's mental health. Paul is simply assuring Timothy that God has equipped us with the power and love to overcome anxiety and self-consciousness so that when speaking to others we can think in a disciplined manner and express ourselves clearly.

If you are self-conscious, God did not make you this way. The roots of your self-consciousness lie deep in your past. Self-conscious children are raised by parents who are difficult to please.

This is the kind of parent who responds to a report card of four A's and a B, by ignoring the A's and asking the child, "Why the B?" Children living in such a home often feel observed, but very seldom feel approved. Parental approval always seems to be just beyond their reach.

How can we deal with this crippling form of anxiety?

First, remember you were not born self-conscious. You learned to be self-conscious early in life from repeated experiences of feeling that you fell short of the approval of those you sought to please. This may not be what they intended, but it was what you learned from them.

Second, remind yourself that your heavenly Father is not hard to please. In the oldest book of the

Bible God leaves no doubt about how pleased he was with Job's life.[10] Sadly, at the time, Job was not aware of this debate. However, the book ends with Satan's defeat and God expressing His pleasure in Job's life.[11]

Often, our image of God is so embedded in other authority figures in our history that we assume He must be more difficult to please than they were because He is the ultimate authority figure. But your heavenly Father does not want you to be timid or self-conscious because you fear His disapproval.

God does not want us to spend our lives trying to avoid His wrath. He wants to relieve us of this kind of fear and anxiety. God loves you and me. He gave His Son, Jesus Christ, for us. On the cross Jesus took our sins and paid the penalty for them. When we accept His death as payment for our sins, the righteousness of Christ's life is credited to our account. Our heavenly Father is pleased with us because He sees in us the righteousness of Christ.[12] Think of that!

Third, remember Jesus' yoke is easy and His burden is light. Jesus did not say, "Come unto me, all you that labor and are heavy laden and I will give you a nervous breakdown." He said, "Come to me, all you who are weary and burdened, and I will give you rest. Take my yoke upon you, and learn from me; for I am gentle and humble in heart, and you will find rest for your souls. For my yoke is easy, and my burden is light."[13]

God gives His children power.

Paul told Timothy that God has given us power, not fear and self-consciousness. What kind of power has God given to us? First of all, God has given us the power to be called His children.[14] The Greek word John uses for power is "exousia," which literally means "authority." So, God has given us the authority to become His children.

The second kind of power God gives the Christian is defined by the Greek word "zoe." The English translation of this word is "everlasting life" or "eternal life."[15] This is the same power by which Christ, as the Word, made all things out of nothing! This power can provide us with creative urges, fantasies, and ideas for meeting the practical decision-making problem-solving challenges we face in our lives every day. Becoming aware of these divine suggestions can be the source of wisdom and creativity for us.

The third kind of power God gives us is expressed by the Greek word "dunamis." Jesus told His disciples, "But you will receive power when the Holy Spirit comes on you: and you will be my witnesses in Jerusalem, and in all Judea and Samaria, and to the ends of the earth."[16]

This Greek word is the source of our English words "dynamo" and "dynamite." Both of these words are energy-related. A dynamo provides a continual flow of energy. Dynamite is expressed in a sudden burst of energy.

In giving this power to believers, Jesus provides the energy required for them to be effective witnesses to the good news of His love. Sometimes this power is expressed in sudden bursts of divine energy as in miracles, signs, and healings, but usually it is a continual flow of unselfish works of love that identify us as children of God. The purpose of these works is to display the life and ministry of Christ in ways that bring peace and joy to others.

God watches you with loving eyes.

As a boy Isaac Watts lived next door to an elderly Christian lady who took a special interest in him. He sensed her love for him, so he visited her often.

One day, she noticed how fascinated Isaac was with a Scripture motto on her wall. It was out of Hagar's prayer in the desert after she was cast out of Abram's home. This brief motto simply said, "Thou God seest me."[17]

Seeing his interest in it, the old lady decided to give this motto to Isaac. As she took it down from the wall and handed it to him she said, "Son, I want you to have this. When you get older, you'll meet people who will read this Scripture on your wall and want to make you believe that it means God is always following you with a judgmental eye, watching you everywhere you go; seeing everything you do; and, searching for some reason to condemn you. Don't you believe that! For what this passage really means is that God loves you so much He just can't take His eyes off of you."

How to conquer unhealthy fears

Many adults tend to be phobic about some things. For example, some people don't like to ride in elevators. They suffer intense anxiety when they are confined in small spaces. This reaction is known as claustrophobia.

Isn't it interesting to watch what people do on elevators? They seldom look at others. They look at the ceiling. They look at the floor. They look at the wall. But we gladly suffer this violation of our spatial boundaries for the convenience of avoiding the stairs.

Then, there's acrophobia—fear of high places. Once in a while, I have a bout with this. I get curious about what it might feel like to jump. That feeling so frightens me that I move away from the edge or railing. This gives me a little taste of what it must be like for people who suffer crippling phobias.

Unhealthy fears have to be faced to be conquered. Adults have few specific fears. Our fears are usually more general. They are more anxiety-provoking than frightening. Talking in front of people or meeting new people can make us anxious. Fear of failing and fear of rejection are also sources of anxiety for us. So, let's take a look at four ways we can deal with this unhealthy fear and anxiety.

1. Learn the value of deep-breathing exercises.

God gave you lungs for specific purposes. Sighs and deep breaths are not simply unconscious reactions to life stress. They are nature's ways of relieving anxiety. Much relief can come to you in anxious moments through deep-breathing exercises.

When doing these exercises, follow this simple routine:

1. Sit comfortably with your back against some support and your feet flat on the floor.
2. Fold your hands across your lap and begin to take your pulse.
   (Put your left index and middle fingers on your wrist just under your right thumb. You should be able to feel your heart beat.)
3. Breathe in slowly for six pulse beats.
4. Breathe out slowly for six pulse beats.
5. Hold your breath for six pulse beats.

Complete these steps three times.[18]

After you have finished this routine just close your eyes and let your shoulders and head drop slightly forward. See how relaxed you feel? This simple exercise will help you reduce stress and lower your anxiety level.

You can even do deep-breathing exercises on the job. When you are anxious, take advantage of your breaks to get the privacy you need and do some deep-breathing exercises. It will give you relief.

2. Apply some rational controls.

You can think yourself out of much fear and anxiety. Learn to subject these uncomfortable emotions to the law of averages. Ask yourself, "What are the chances that what I fear will actually happen? What are the statistical odds my fears will come true?"

If you are a habitual worrier this may not help you. You may be like the man who stood on the street corner snapping his fingers for hours. Someone finally went up to him and said, "For some time, I've been watching you stand here on the corner snapping your fingers. I'm curious. What does that do for you?"

"Oh," the man replied, "If you keep it a secret I'll tell you. I'm terrified of elephants, and I'm doing my best to keep them away from me."

Hoping to relieve the poor man, his observer replied, "Sir, don't you know there isn't an elephant within 2000 miles of this place?" "Yeah," the finger snapper said gleefully, "you see, it works!"

Some people are convinced worrying works. Others have been brave enough to discover that the chance their worries will materialize is so small that it doesn't pay to worry. Paul shares this bit of practical wisdom with his readers: "Do not be anxious about anything, but in everything, by prayer and petition, with thanksgiving, present your requests to God. And the peace of God, which transcends all understanding, will guard your hearts and your minds in Christ Jesus."[19]

Statistical perspective

Try as we will, none of us can take all of the risk out of living. Living is risk-taking. But learning not to exaggerate your risks can lower your anxiety level. Putting some statistical perspective on our fears helps to weaken their grip on us.[20]

For example, when you compare the number of automobile accidents with the number of drivers and automobiles on the highway there is little likelihood of you being involved in a life threatening automobile accident. Or, if you compare the total number of people who shop at convenience stores with the number of patrons who will witness a robbery, there is a very small chance that you will face such a frightening experience.

Do you fear other people won't like you?

The use of statistical perspective is also an effective way of managing our fear that other people won't like us. As with other unhealthy fears, this one also has to be faced to be conquered. You might begin to manage it by asking yourself, "What are the chances that everyone I meet will like me?" An honest response to that question requires each of us to admit, "Zero."

Then proceed to ask yourself, "Why should everyone like me?" Isn't that expecting too much of people? To expect everyone to like me is insinuating that there is nothing about me that is not likeable. So, I am content with the number of people who dislike me and grateful that others don't know as much about me as I know about myself. If they did I'm sure the number of people who dislike me would increase considerably.

Not everyone loved Jesus. Even among the twelve who were closest to Him there were two He couldn't count on—one denied Him and the other betrayed Him. That is approximately 16 percent of the disciples. You see, Jesus could only depend on about 85 percent of His disciples to display their love for Him.

It would be nice if everyone loved us, but is it really necessary? If seven or eight out of every ten people you meet like you, isn't that enough? With odds like that in your favor when you meet new people, why not assume they will like you and be surprised when they don't. This mental posture will help you feel much more comfortable around people and increase the chances that they will find you likable.

3. Learn to meditate on Bible scenes.

When you are anxious or afraid, meditate on some of your favorite Bible scenes. The Word of God is filled with passages depicting restful, relaxing scenes upon which you can meditate. Often, when we are anxious, calm can be restored through the effective use of this kind of mental imagery.

Because Hindus and Buddhists place such great emphasis on this form of prayer many Christians have felt it is inappropriate for them to practice meditation. Some have even been fearful of it. It puts you in touch with the spiritual source of your faith. For the Christian that source is the God of the Bible. Meditation has always been an important form of Judeo-Christian prayer. David says of the blessed man that: " . . . his delight is in the law of the Lord, and on his law he meditates day and night."[21]

Meditation minimizes fear and maximizes faith.

From the moment Gail left her house she was frightened. Driving on the expressway to keep her appointments with me was so terrifying for her she had to depend on someone else to drive her to the sessions. She was an attractive, intelligent Christian woman in her late 40's but seriously crippled by anxiety.

In getting acquainted with Gail, I discovered she was very imaginative. Most people who are anxious and fearful have active imaginations, but they are focused on the wrong kind of mental images. Wanting her to discover how her imagination could work for her rather than against her, I asked, "Gail, what are your three favorite

Bible scenes?" She listed them without hesitation: "The Twenty-third Psalm, the Good Shepherd and the one lost sheep, and Jesus calming the storm on Lake Galilee."

"Good," I said. "Now, I want these scenes to become so real to you that they minister to you. First, I want you to take three deep breaths." When she had finished her deep breathing exercises she dropped her shoulders and closed her eyes. Then, I suggested, "While your eyes are closed and you are enjoying such a good relaxed feeling, picture in your mind the Bible scene you like most. When you have it in focus, tell me which one it is and describe it for me"

Gail's first choice was the Twenty-third Psalm. She worked with that scene until she could picture the green pastures, see the surrounding hills, hear the rippling waters of the stream, the sounds of the shepherd's staff and the bleating of the sheep. With very little effort, she also developed the ability to fix her other favorite Bible scenes in her imagination.

Gail was instructed to take a few moments before leaving the house to recreate one of those scenes in her mind. Then I reminded her that each of them emphasized the reality of Christ's presence with her everywhere she went. Teaching Gail to meditate on the Lord and on the Word brought a major breakthrough in her battle for sanity.

By beginning to focus on an awareness of God's presence and assuring herself that she could do all things through Christ, Gail was able to drive to her sessions after the first five weeks of treatment. She was also able to meet friends at the mall and enjoy shopping with them.

4. Focus on reassuring passages of Scripture.

Practice recalling and meditating on reassuring passages of Scripture. Here are some examples:

"Peace I leave with you, my peace I give you. I do

not give to you as the world gives. Do not let your hearts be troubled and do not be afraid."[22]

"Fear not, for I am with you; be not dismayed, for I am your God. I will strengthen you, Yes, I will help you, I will uphold you with my righteous right hand."[23]

"...He that is in you is greater than he that is in the world."[24]

"I can do everything through him who gives me strength."[25]

"And we know that in all things God works together for the good of those that love him, who have been called according to his purpose."[26]

"What, then shall we say in response to this? If God is for us, who can be against us?"[27]

Don't panic!

Seeing angels in the middle of the night on a lonely hillside in Bethlehem must have been very frightening for the shepherds. So, before the angel of the Lord announced Christ's birth to them, He said, "Do not be afraid."[28] Why did he say that? He had come to give them detailed information about where they could find baby Jesus, and he wanted to be sure they remembered it.

Can you imagine how you would feel if you had been among those shepherds that night? Initially, I would have been paralyzed by fear. Had the angel of the Lord not helped them manage their fear, they never would have remembered where to find the Christ child. Fear fogs your memory. When we are being overwhelmed by fear and anxiety we miss the creative options God is giving us for the problem-solving decision-making challenges of life. Determine to confront the sources of crippling fear and anxiety in your life. Begin by applying some of the suggestions found in this chapter. Some of your fears you may conquer almost instantly. However, others you will overcome more gradually.

Learning to come to terms with fears and anxieties will help you become more confident in your approach to life. This may put you in touch with angry feelings you have been too anxious to acknowledge. Anger makes a good servant, but a poor master. In the next chapter I will suggest some practical ways for getting in touch with your angry feelings and putting them to work for you!

Discussion Questions

1. In what ways can fear and anxiety be healthy?
2. When do our fears and anxieties become unhealthy?
3. Where do our fears come from?
4. What is meant by the term boundaries?
5. Why is it important to set physical, social, and spiritual boundaries for our lives? Read Proverbs 29:18 again and discuss its connection with the concept of boundaries.
6. In what ways can fear and anxiety be detrimental to us physically and emotionally?
7. What are some of the natural controls for anxiety that God has given us?
8. What is the statistical perspective method of controlling fear?
9. How can focusing on reassuring passages of Scripture help alleviate fear and anxiety? Give specific examples of helpful passages?
10. Discuss the connection of 2 Timothy 1:7 with self-consciousness.

FOOTNOTES

[1] President Franklin D. Roosevelt's First Inaugural Address, in **Lend Me Your Ears**: Company: New York, N. Y., 1997, p.859.

[2] Genesis 3:8-10

[3] I John 4:18

[4] Luke 8:50; 12:32

[5] Proverbs 9:10

[6] Revelation 13:16-18

[7] Luke 12:10

[8] 2 Timothy 1:5

[9] 2 Timothy 1:7

[10] Job 1:9

[11] Job 42:12-17

[12] 2 Corinthians 5:21

[13] Matthew 11:28-30

[14] John 1:12

[15] 1 John 5:11-12

[16] Acts 1:8

[17] Genesis 16:13

[18] Remulla, Rosalyn. **Decrease anxiety from stress in the office: use deep breathing;** www.ags.uci.edu/~coiet-tem/remuiia/paper.html; 6/30/2002.

[19] Philippians 4:6-7

[20] Goleman, Daniel. **Emotional Intelligence**, New York: Bantam Books, 1995, p.65.

[21] Psalms 1:2

[22] John 14:27

[23] Isaiah 41:10

[24] I John 4:4

[25] Philippians 4:13

[26] Romans 8:28

[27] Romans 8:31

[28] Luke 2:10

CHAPTER FIVE

ANGER:
MASTER
OR
SERVANT?

I couldn't believe what I was seeing. My wife and I were on our way to church when there in a parked car on the side of the road a small-framed woman was draped over the front seat and a man twice her size was brutally beating her.

We were horrified! Immediately, the parable of the Good Samaritan came to my mind and I realized I had to do something. A traffic circle was just ahead of us and a police car was passing me in the opposite direction so I flagged him down.

While I was telling the officer what we had seen, the man had pulled his car back onto the highway and was proceeding toward the traffic circle. We watched as he pulled into a gas station.

The officer asked my wife and me to jump in the cruiser with him. He turned the cruiser around and sped toward the gas station pulling in immediately in front of the man's car so there was no risk of him fleeing. The woman got out of the car and headed for the ladies room to clean herself up. When I saw how bloody she was it made me sick.

The officer angrily confronted the man, "You must be proud of yourself after doing such a manly thing like that to your wife." "She's not my wife. She's my mother," the man sullenly replied. "It's a good thing for you that I'm in uniform," the officer countered.

By this time the older woman approached her son's car pleading with the officer not to arrest him. "You can't

do anything to him if I don't press charges," she said.
"After all, he's only doing what he saw his father do many
times."

The officer explained to her that her son had made
the mistake of doing this in public and that as an officer of
the law he was going to press charges. He called a cab to
take the old woman home and a tow truck to impound the
man's car. I can't tell you how satisfying it was for my
wife and I to see the man handcuffed and headed for jail.

This story proves again that – for better or for
worse– modeling is the most powerful form of teaching.
Most often, abusers of women are raised in the homes of
abusers of women. The way children express anger is
highly likely to be an imitation of the way adults around
them talk and act when they get angry.

This is not a new problem in our society. The
national scope of domestic violence has been known for a
long time. Almost three decades ago the Joint
Commission on the Mental Health of Children said:

> The role of violence and its encouragement in
> young children must be faced squarely. Some
> children meet abuse and angry out bursts at
> the hand of their parents. Nearly all children
> are exposed to graphic violence over the tele-
> vision screen. Through possible imitation of
> and identification with these models, patterns
> of violent behavior may be easily acquired.
> Of at least equal importance are the patterns
> by which the young child is taught to handle
> his own frustrations, his own angry feelings,
> and the constructive or destructive acts for
> which he comes to feel responsible. Possibly
> no other area repre sents as profound a source
> of pathology in our culture as the handling of
> anger and aggression.[1]

Few parents teach their children approved ways of expressing anger. And the church offers very little help in this area. In fact, church people frequently see any expression of anger as being at least undesirable, if not downright sinful. Many Christians incorrectly believe anger is the result of the fall of mankind.

However, God created Adam and Eve as emotional beings. He gave them the ability to experience anger and express aggression. These were essential if they were to carry out there divine commission: ". . . fill the earth, and subdue it."[2]

Adam and Eve were to subdue the earth and have dominion over it. An anger drive and the ability to be aggressive were essential for this task. After all, passive people will never subdue anything. Anger and aggression were part of the original emotional equipment God gave Adam and Eve for carrying out their task. When anger is experienced and expressed in healthy ways it can provide the intensity and energy for an effective life.

Our battle with anger begins early.

As soon as parental love relieves us of infant fears, each of us becomes secure enough to demonstrate anger. Any mother knows what infant rage is. Once her soft, tender little bundle of love stiffens, reddens, and screams, she knows he has begun his lifelong bout with anger. What triggers off this anger? The limits parents begin to set on their infant's behavior.

These limits inevitably frustrate the baby. If he has been loved enough to feel secure, he will vent his frustration in an angry test of those limits. Learning to manage such angry moments in ways that meet with his parents' approval is essential to the child's survival.

Babies soon learn parents don't want them to get angry. However, few parents are thoughtful enough to teach their children approved ways of expressing anger. As a result, children often learn to feel guilty or even sinful for experiencing anger, but they don't learn how to master it.

Children raised in Christian families are subject to less violence in their homes, but they probably receive no more positive training in dealing with anger than their peers who are raised in secular families. If this statement startles you, remember that for some Christians being angry is the same as being "bad."

For many Christians anger, in legal terms, is not only a misdemeanor, it's a felony. They cannot bring themselves to admit that they are angry even when their anger is obvious to others.

"Yes you are!" "No I'm not!" "Yes you are!"

Those who see anger as inconsistent with their faith must either deny their anger or confess it as sin. Unfortunately, it is much easier to deny it. So, those who are uncomfortable admitting their anger find other words to describe the same feeling. They can say that they are terribly upset, nervous, frustrated, irritated, disappointed or even furious much more easily than they can admit to being angry.

Can you imagine how ridiculous it must be to observe two friends like this engaging in a heated argument? As the conflict increases, voices are raised, the muscles stand out in one's neck, and a sharp edge comes into his voice. His face reddens—and then his more spiritual friend says condescendingly, "My brother, you're angry!" And the other shouts back, "I am not angry!"

Of course, any neutral observer of such a confrontation realizes that both men are extremely angry. Admitting it, however, would leave them feeling guilty because of their mutual deeply rooted conviction that "good Christians" don't get angry.

If parents feel this way about anger their response when their children become angry is likely to be more punitive and suppressive than instructive. However, the Bible does not present such a recriminating view of anger.

The Bible speaks openly about anger.

David reveals that *"God is a righteous judge who expresses his wrath every day."*[3]

Even Jesus knew what it meant to be angry. And He expressed it in church! One Sabbath when Jesus was in the synagogue the Pharisees were looking for some reason to condemn Him so they tried to trick Him into breaking the Sabbath.

A man was there with a shriveled hand. The Pharisees believed healing this man would be a violation of their law forbidding any work on the Sabbath that was not absolutely essential. So, they watched to see if Jesus would heal this man.

It was obvious that the Pharisees were more interested in tricking Jesus into breaking their law than they were in helping this poor, crippled man. Such a perversion of the law angered Jesus. So, He decided to heal the man to spite them.

Here's how Mark describes it. "Another time he went into the synagogue; and a man with a shriveled hand was there. Some of them were looking for a reason to accuse Jesus, so they watched him closely to see if he would heal him on the Sabbath day. Jesus said to the man with the shriveled hand, 'Stand up in front of everyone.' Then Jesus asked them, 'Which is lawful on the Sabbath: to do good or to do evil, to save life, or to kill?' But they remained silent. He had looked round at them with anger and, deeply distressed at their stubborn hearts, said to the man, 'Stretch out your hand.' He stretched it out, and his hand was completely restored. Then the Pharisees went out, and began to plot with the Herodians how they might kill Jesus."[4]

Anger is a normal human emotion.

If God expresses His wrath every day and even Jesus experienced anger, then maybe our fear of our own anger and subsequent guilt for expressing it are exaggerated reactions to a normal human emotion. To help you deal with your fear of anger, I want to share with you a simple "**ABCD**" formula for appropriately managing it. By putting this formula into practice you and others can live more comfortably with your anger.

"A" - Accept anger as a fact of your life.

Like the common cold, anger is a recurrent life experience. You may not like it, but you can't ignore it and stay healthy. Resolutions about never becoming angry again only pile on more guilt the next time you are angry—so forget them!

Anger is the second emotion we learn to experience; only fear precedes it. When we experience anger as an infant no guilt is associated with it. We *learn* to feel guilty for being angry. However, most of us were taught to feel guilty about our anger so early in life that we cannot remember a time when we didn't.

Of course, when expressions of anger are undisciplined and destructive, it is healthy to feel guilty. All of us should be concerned about the dangerous side effects of undisciplined anger. Paul addresses this concern when writing to the Ephesians: "Do not let the sun go down while you are still angry."[5]

Unfortunately, instead of seeing this as a command from Paul to learn healthy ways of managing anger, many people see it as implying that if you are a good Christian you never get angry. Actually, Paul is saying that as long as we are human we will have to come to terms with anger. He is urging us to learn how to manage it promptly, effectively, and constructively. Once we are able to do that, we no longer need to be afraid of our anger or guilty for experiencing it. Then, with the Lord's help, we can put each day's conflicts to rest with the sunset.

The apostles creatively managed anger.

There are few subjects that stir the emotions more than religious differences. And, the issues they were discussing at the Council of Jerusalem were major issues. How much of the Jewish law, if any, should Gentile Christians be required to keep? This was the topic at the Council of Jerusalem. These issues were so deep that they caused great discomfort and embarrassment between Paul and Peter even after the Council of Jerusalem.[6]

Can you imagine the apostles arguing and debating these differences between the leaders of the Jewish and Gentile Christians without raising their voices? Recording that historic event, Luke honestly acknowledges that the agreement reached only came about after there had been " . . . much disputing."[7]

It would stretch one's credibility if he were to imply that an extended debate over such contentious issues could proceed without a clash of impassioned and sometimes angry emotions. Yet, the participants in this heated debate were not only "good Christians," they were apostles and elders of the church.[8] There is no hint that this intense exchange of sharp differences was a negative reflection on their spirituality. This is an excellent Biblical illustration of the creative management of conflict.

The fact that you experience anger in no way implies that you should consider yourself less spiritual than others. It is far healthier to view anger as a normal human emotion that everyone must learn to deal with daily than to pretend that it doesn't exist in the life of the "good" Christian. You can assume this attitude much more easily if you begin to see anger for what it really is.

Anger is unexpressed energy.

Physiologically, this is exactly what it is. When your mind interprets some situation as threatening or intimidating, a biochemical reaction is triggered which results in the creation of unusually large amounts of energy for use in facing the threat.

Think for a moment of what that means. Under certain conditions matter can be destroyed—but energy cannot be destroyed; it can only be transformed. So, once you are angry you are in possession of energy that cannot be destroyed.

Until you determine what form the expression of this energy will take, you have committed no sin. Your moral challenge is to responsibly determine what you will do with the energy your anger has created.

If a person can't admit he is angry, he will have great difficulty learning healthy ways of discharging this energy. Therefore, the first step in our formula for anger management is simply to accept anger as a fact of your life. Realize that there is no reason for you to experience guilt or shame so long as you express you anger appropriately.

Anger appears at unexpected times.

Once you are able to accept your anger, you may find it showing up at unexpected times. Often when people are grieving, they are aware of anger. They may feel so embarrassed and guilty about this that they can't discuss it even with their closest friend. Yet this is such a common experience that few people suffer the loss of loved ones without going through it.

In moments like this your anger may not make sense to you, nevertheless it is real. Sometimes you are angry with your loved one for dying and leaving you. You may be angry with the medical team for not being able to save your loved one. At times you may be angry with God for permitting the events to happen.

How should we cope in these circumstances? First, be assured that these feelings are common among people going through similar experiences. Then, express your anger to God. You may discover this to be very difficult for you because we often fear that if we express anger to God, He will get angry with us.

Some of us have vivid mental pictures of how angry our parents became with us when we were children. If this was your experience, remind yourself that your heavenly Father is not like your earthly parent who may have responded to your anger by becoming furious with you.

"B" - Become aware of your anger.

Unrecognized anger is far more dangerous to us than anger we are prepared to accept and recognize. When you learn to accept your anger, no one has to tell you that you're angry. You are aware of it. You know you're angry.

When you know that you are angry, you can choose from among several healthy and appropriate ways of expressing it. However, if you insist on denying your anger, when it finally breaks through your defenses you are likely to express it in ways that embarrass you and damage your relationships with important people in your life.

Getting in touch with feelings is difficult for men.
Our culture unintentionally brutalizes males.
Often, as little boys we are taught to grow calluses on our
feelings. So, when we grow up we are at a real disadvan-
tage in recognizing and talking about them.

For example, when a little girl falls down, skins her
knee and comes crying to Mother or Dad for comfort she
is taken up in their arms, given some affection, and assured
that everything will be all right. When her little brother
falls down and comes running to their parents expecting
the same treatment the parent may take him by the shoulder and say something like: "Hey, hey, big guy...you're
okay. Be tough! No need to cry over a little skin off the
knee...be Daddy's big man!"

In such informal ways as this, boys learn that a
man in our culture is not expected to show his emotions.
We expect our men to be "tough." Unfortunately, part of
being tough or strong means learning to be insensitive to
emotional pain. This is a part of the male's traditional
preparation for bearing the brunt of our nation's military
obligation and job market stress in our highly competitive
society.

These differences in the way males and females are
socialized are widely recognized. In fact, they become
part of our national sense of humor. For example, men
may jokingly remark that the woman's motto is, "If at first
you don't succeed, cry, cry again!"

Take a personal safari!
Becoming aware of anger in your life may require
you to go on a search for it. So, begin to look for the
places in your life where you think you may be unconsciously hiding anger.

Look underneath idiomatic expressions often used
to disguise anger. Catch yourself saying things like: "I'm

fed up." "I've had it." "I'm sick and tired of that." "That burns me up." "I can't swallow that." "He makes me sick." "She makes me sick to my stomach." "I'm disgusted." "You make me laugh."

What about this one? "I'm hurt." We won't permit our patients to say they are hurt unless they are willing to say that they are angry. After all, do you think it is possible for someone to hurt you without making you angry?

Many of my patients resist acknowledging the association between pain and anger. They will say, "I'm just so hurt." But I will insist, "And angry." "Oh, no!" they object. "I'm not angry—I'm just hurt."

Then I explain, "If someone came in here and hit me in the face I can predict that two feelings would surface simultaneously in me. One would be pain. The other would be anger. Yes, I would be hurt—but I also would be angry. Don't just recognize one of those feelings—acknowledge them both!"

Usually the person will say, "Well, when you put it that way, I can see what you're talking about. I guess I'm hurt and angry."

Don't hide your anger from yourself.

Unfortunately, the church has allowed people to identify with the pain of a hurtful experience but not with the anger: it is alright for believers to say, "I'm hurt," but it's not okay for them to say, "I'm angry."

As a result of this kind of religious training, it is extremely difficult for people to say they are angry when their children are living contrary to the way they have been raised. Instead, they say, "My children are breaking my heart."

Who are we kidding? Of course, once in a while our children behave in ways that hurt us. But I can tell you without any hesitation that when my children hurt me they also ticked me off. When they behaved in ways that made me look like a failure as a parent, I was not only hurt—I was angry.

I was smart enough not to tell my friends that I was angry with my child. I told them that I was very concerned for my child. Or, if I wanted to appear even more spiritual, I would say, "My child is breaking my heart." Of course, there's nothing wrong with simply sharing the pain of our parental experiences with our friends. We should know ourselves well enough, however, to know that anger is mixed in with the pain and sadness we are experiencing. Even though you may feel it is socially desirable to hide this from others, don't hide it from yourself. You can deal with anger more effectively once you recognize it is there. Become aware of your anger!

Look for anger in episodes of depression.

Depression is another hiding place for anger. More frequently than not, situational depression is aggravated if not initially caused by anger unconsciously turned inward as a form of self-hatred. However, depressed people seldom recognize themselves as being angry. They say things like, "I feel blue." "I'm really down." "I wish I were dead." "Sometimes I just feel like killing myself."

It never ceases to amaze me that people can be suicidal and still deny that they are angry. In an effort to put these desperate people in touch with their anger, I have said to them, "It must be very painful to be so angry with yourself," and had them reply in genuine amazement, "What makes you think I am angry?"

Sometimes I have been successful in helping such a person see his hidden anger by saying something like, "Well, I've always believed that before you could bring yourself to kill someone you had to be very angry with him—even if that someone happens to be you." Seeing

these people get in touch with their anger toward themselves for the first time is very interesting.

Once the person recognizes their anger and begins
to be aware of it, they have taken an important step toward
recovery. We'll pursue a more complete discussion of
anger's role in depression in a later chapter.

Living with a depressed person can be anger-provoking.

Years ago, my first wife battled postpartum depression after the birth of our first child. I didn't understand
what she was going through. All I knew was that I would
come home day after day and find her depressed. I didn't
know how to give her the emotional support she needed.
I'm sure this must have been frustrating for her.

Out of the frustration of coming home and finding
her depressed again I would say really brilliant things like,
"Oh, no, not again!" Or, worse yet, "Honey, you know, I
don't know what to do. I try and try to be the best husband I can, but it doesn't seem to help."

Both of these statements are full of anger. I wonder how I could have been so blind to it. Unconsciously I
suppose I was trying to get my wife to hide her depression
from me so I wouldn't have to deal with the overwhelming feeling of powerlessness it generated in me. I guess I
was hoping she would feel so guilty for being depressed
that she would somehow just snap out of it.

"They shall be comforted."

Then one day when I found her on the verge of
tears, the Holy Spirit prompted me to put my arms around
her, tuck her head on my shoulder, and say to her, "Honey,
go ahead and let your feelings out. You'll feel better when
you've cried and gotten your feelings out of you."

Immediately she began to sob her heart out. I
hadn't said anything magical, but when she was finished

crying she had gotten some of her feelings out of her. She not only felt better, but I had grown considerably taller in her estimation, because I had learned to communicate with her at an emotional level.

My anger had been provoked by feelings of power-lessness in responding to my wife's depression. Finding a way of offering her some relief for her depression chan-neled the energy created by my anger into a helpful ges-ture of compassion, took the edge off my frustration and left me with the good feeling of having done something that helped my wife.

Look for your anger in your nonverbal behavior.

If you want to become aware of your anger learn to look for it in places where it may be hiding. Are you an angry driver? How fierce are you in competitive sports? How do you react when your side loses in party games? How much do you grind your teeth? How do you manage it when someone keeps you waiting?

Get curious about where your anger may be hiding from you. You are much more likely to manage it mature-ly if you discover it early in its inception. This will allow you to work at controlling your anger before you are over-whelmed by it.

"Oh, my aching back!"

Since anger affects you physiologically, get curious about where its presence may be announced in your body. What happens to you physically when you get angry? Where does your body first express anger?

I can feel my neck muscles tighten. My shoulders get tense. A sharp edge can be heard in my voice. People literally give me a pain in the neck.

Where do you experience anger? Some people first become aware of it in the cardiovascular area. Others develop lower back pain. Some experience anger in the gastrointestinal tract. Others have difficulty breathing.

Ask yourself what happens in your body when you become angry. Where do you feel it? The earlier and more precisely you detect your anger the more effective you will be at imposing controls for it.

This brings us to the third step in our formula:

"C" - Control your anger.

Accepting anger as a normal part of life and detecting its early physical presence in your body gains you the advance notice needed to control it. This can save you from the embarrassment of undisciplined displays of anger.

Our maturity is measured by our ability to accept our emotions, become aware of them, and control them in socially appropriate ways. The mature person is in touch with his or her feelings and has control of them. A person's spiritual maturity can be measured by the size of the things that make him or her angry. The more spiritually mature a person is the higher tolerance they will have for frustration.

If you do not learn to control your anger as a single person then angry moments in marriage will be much more difficult for you. In this most intimate of relationships you will not only have your own angry feelings to contend with at times, but you also will have to deal with your partner's anger.

When you see your mate out of control there are a number of things you can do. First of all, determine if the anger is directed at you. If it isn't, then help your mate vent his anger by supporting him in the process. Saying things like: "I don't blame you. That would get under my skin, too." "I can see why you feel that way." "You wouldn't be human if that didn't upset you."

This kind of support will help your mate verbalize his feelings. Often, just a sympathetic hearing will bring relief from his anger. Being there for him will also strengthen his love and appreciation for you.

If his anger is directed at you, try to understand what you have said or done to anger your mate. Many times, he has misunderstood your intention. In that event an honest explanation helps to clear the air.

If you have said or done things that were inconsiderate, apologize. Arguments can be shortened and peace restored quickly by simply saying, "I'm sorry, dear. Please forgive me."

You need to develop a number of strategies for dealing with times when both of you are angry. If the anger is so intense you interrupt each other in your hurry to see who can say the most cruel things to each other you need to learn the discipline of "time out." Both of you will need to give each other space and time for your emotions to subside. You can go to different rooms. You can take a walk. Any activity that is safe can serve as a buffer that allows the two of you to regain control of your emotions. However, eventually you will have to deal with the issues that provoked your anger. In doing so, many couples have found the following formula to be helpful:

Four rules to fight by:
1. Stick to the subject. Agree to stay with the issues creating your conflict. It is easy to allow the heat of the moment to provoke you into revisiting all of the tender places in your marital history.

2. Don't fight dirty. Develop the discipline of refusing to use words that are designed primarily to hurt your spouse. Stay away from those sharp remarks that flail each others' egos. Sometimes I remind couples, "Your mouth is like a shotgun. Once you pull the trigger, it's hard to put the pieces back together." Your spouse will never need to forget something you've been wise enough NOT to say.

3. Learn how to compromise. Staying flexible and learning how to negotiate are keys to resolving conflict. Remember, it's no fun to be married to someone who has to win every argument. Getting beyond the discomfort of the moment and arriving with as few wounds as possible is a desirable goal.

4. Stay good humored. It's difficult, if not impossible, to be good humored in the middle of an argument. However, as you look back over the things that have angered you in the past you can see how ridiculous many of them were. These are the stories that can provide a lot of holiday humor for you and your family.

Parents also get angry.

At times, our children also can push most of us beyond our limits. The best thing to do when you "lose it" with one of your children is to apologize to the child. Children are among the world's most forgiving people. And, the humiliation of asking your child to forgive you should help you have better control of your anger in the future. Your honesty in apologizing to your child also sets a good precedent for requiring the child to apologize to other family members when he or she has lost his or her temper.

There's a place for healthy anger in parenthood. Just stay in control of it. Remaining calm and unruffled when your children are misbehaving in embarrassing ways requires a level of sainthood most of us never reach. However, be sure the issues that have upset you are big enough to justify the anger you feel.

Don't create a major scene over minor offenses.

The following story beautifully illustrates this

point. A mother heard her four-year-old son screaming and crying from the basement where he was watching his father build cupboards. Fearing the boy had been seriously hurt, she opened the basement door and saw him sitting on the steps sobbing his little heart out.

"Honey, what in the world is wrong with you?" she demanded. Through his tears the little fellow volunteered, "Daddy hit his thumb with the hammer."

"Well, if daddy hit his thumb with the hammer, then why are you crying?" she asked. "Well . . . I didn't cry at first," her son admitted. "I laughed."

In homes like this children soon discover what they cannot do when their parents are angry. However, they may get very little help in learning what they can do when they are angry.

In helping your children deal with their anger, remember the difference between "motes" and "beams."[9] Don't use parental cannons to hunt for children's gnats. Such an exaggerated approach may win the battle, but it often results in you losing the war. They concede to your wishes, but you lose their respect.

Teenagers can be especially challenging to a parent's anger management. They argue so eloquently. If you are not careful they will goad you into a shouting match over a very minor point. However, once tempers are ignited a major battle is waged.

When a parent has to get into a shouting match with a teenager it is an indication that the parent's case is weak. If your case is strong enough, you don't need to shout to make it stick.

Keeping your "cool" can be a challenge.

If you want to feel what it is like to have someone's passive aggression aimed at you, put yourself in this father's place. The family had been seated at the table several minutes waiting for the oldest son to take his place. At last, he rushed into the dining room. He sat down at the table and bowed his head. His father noticed that the boy's hands were filthy.

He said to his son, "You know better than to come to the table with hands like that. Get upstairs and wash your hands." The family waited patiently for him.

Finally, after several more minutes, his father shouted, "What's taking you so long?" The son replied whiningly, "I'm only doing what you told me to do."

For a parent not to feel provoked by that kind of behavior is asking too much. However, a wise parent will learn not to fall into that kind of trap, lose his cool, and lash out at the child.

It will take practice to refuse the bait. But the first time you succeed you will feel wonderful. Get wise to the tactics of your teenagers. Be sure your case is strong and fair. Once you know you are fair, then be firm—and be friendly.

God wants the energy created by your anger to be expressed constructively. If putting your anger into constructive action is a problem for you, let me give you some simple rules that will help you get on top of this challenge.

Anger makes a poor master.

Uncontrolled or misdirected anger can be our worst enemy. It can complicate or even destroy one's life. Anger does more harm to the human heart than any other emotion.

For example, among young men preparing to practice medicine, Dr. Redford Williams found those scoring higher on measures of hostility were seven times more likely to have died before the age of 50 than those with low hostility scores. For this group, being quick tempered was a higher predictor of early death than smoking, high blood pressure or high cholesterol.[10]

In addition to the physical threats misguided anger poses, only God knows how many personal lives, marriages, and families have been wrecked by anger gone awry. On the other hand, when anger is properly harnessed it can be turned into a very productive servant. Anyone who wants to can learn how to make anger his or her servant. And, the earlier in life you start the easier the discipline is to learn.

Avoid *clamming up*!

In your efforts to control anger avoid clamming up. People who attempt to control anger by clamming up risk damaging their physical health. Psychosomatic illnesses feed on unexpressed anger. God has not designed your body to accommodate large amounts of unexpressed anger over long periods of time.

As much as possible, the energy created by the anger of the day needs to be released before the day's end. If you don't develop ways of getting that energy out of you, it will find symptomatic expression among the weakest of your organic systems.

So, consciously work at transforming the energy created by angry moments into useful activities that either will help you get your day's agenda done or keep you physically fit. Don't clam up and run the risk of damaging your physical health.

Avoid *blowing up*!

The second way of managing anger is to avoid blowing up. When you blow up, you damage your relationships. If you don't say it, there'll be nothing to forget. If you don't do it, there will be nothing to remember.

There are better ways of managing anger than resorting to these extremes. If you are in control of anger you don't suffer the long-term consequences of it being in control of you.

When your anger gets control of you, you say things and do things that complicate your life. Often, you create circumstances that are difficult, if not impossible, to reverse. Anger, out of control, can destroy your family. Therefore, awareness of our anger becomes important in alerting us to our needs for control.

In His Sermon on the Mount, Jesus makes it clear that the less control a person has over his anger the more serious the consequences he will face: "But I tell you that anyone who is angry with his brother will be subject to judgment. Again, anyone who says to his brother, 'Raca!' is answerable to the Sanhedrin. But anyone who says, 'You fool!' will be in danger of the fire of hell." Notice, if you are angry without a cause you are only in danger of "the judgment."

Once impulse control is lost and the friend is called an idiot, you are in danger of the Sanhedrin. If you curse your brother, then you are "in danger of the fire of hell."[11]

The principle Jesus is teaching here is clear. The less control a person has over his anger, the more serious the consequences he must face. This not only defines the way God deals with us, but it also usually defines the way anger management works in our daily life.

Suggestions for control
First, learn to identify the source of your anger. Are you simply angry at life, or is there someone in particular who has angered you? Are you angry at specific circumstances in your life? What has angered you?

Secondly, determine if the degree of your anger is

justified. If someone else were in the same situation is it likely they would feel the same way?

Apply your controls!

Build up a repertoire of behaviors that seem to work reasonably well for you. Here are some suggestions. Suppose you and you and a friend are in a verbal battle. You have reached that familiar place in your argument where both of you are generating more heat than light. There doesn't seem to be any solution and you can feel yourselves losing control.

At that point, why not take some time out to cool off. A few minutes apart can prevent greater damage to your relationship. After all, if you never speak the words they never have to be forgotten.

Then, put some physical space between the two of you. Go to another room. Change your activity. Get busy doing something that can take your mind off things temporarily. Doing this can help you regain your composure.

You can also try silently counting from one to ten. Often this gives you enough time and emotional distance to overcome your temptation to let your friend have a zinger. Saying the Lord's Prayer to yourself is another way of diverting attention away from the conflict and regaining your self control.[12]

Go for a walk. Notice, I am not suggesting you go for a drive. It is not safe to drive when you are extremely angry. However, going for a walk is an excellent way to cool off. Try any simple behavior that will help you avoid a hasty response you will regret later. Many people would give anything to take back what they said to a friend or family member in a moment of anger.

Assure your friend that your request for "time out" doesn't mean you are trying to avoid the subject of the controversy. If the matter is important enough to produce that much friction then it is too important to postpone indefinitely. However, once both of you establish a track record of good faith by picking up the discussion at a future time when you are in better control, it should be easier to tolerate these delays.

Develop these simple disciplines. They will help you managing intense conflict with your self-respect intact, your anger in control, and your relationship unharmed.

"D" - Direct you anger.

Young children can learn how to redirect the energy produced by their anger more easily than adults. If you have children in the home, give them permission to be angry. However, do not allow them to brood or vent their anger. Brooding adds fuel to the flames of anger. Talking to children and helping them see the anger provoking situation differently can de-escalate their anger. Then, you can give them a choice of energy-demanding activities they can engage in that will not necessarily cost them your approval.

Here are a few suggestions of ways you may permit your children to work off their anger after you have had a constructive talk with them. Allow them to go to their rooms; to play physically demanding games; to write down the reasons why they are angry; to work out on athletic equipment, etc. You can probably come up with a longer list on your own.

The point is that when your children choose to do things you have defined for them to do when they're angry, you should brag on them. Say things to them like, "I know you were very angry this morning, but it was really neat for me to see the way you managed your anger. How did you feel about the way you behaved?"

Then listen to the feedback. It will help you know what they are thinking about as they learn to manage their angry moments. A simple plan like this can help your children grow up having control over their anger most of the time.

There's hope for adults, too!

Your parents may not have taught you positive ways of dealing with anger, but your heavenly Father can help you get in control of it. Anyone who is willing to work at taming his or her anger can count on God's help in the process. Here are four practical steps to follow:

1. Be determined to succeed.

Anger has controlled you long enough. Promise yourself that with God's help you are going to gain control over it. Commitment to succeed is an essential first step in this battle.

2. Sublimate your anger.

In the beginning, realize this is a joint effort between you and God. Remember, the energy created by your anger can be used in many different ways. For example, a regular exercise program will serve the interest of your physical health. And it will help you discharge energy generated in moments of anger. If you prefer more recreational activity, your anger can be expressed in jogging, racquetball, golf, any other sport you may find enjoyable.

The more skilled you become in accepting and detecting your anger, the more capable you will be of putting its energy to healthy use. And, you can become angry with such social issues as illiteracy, poverty, all forms of prejudice, drunken driving, pornography, and TV violence.

These offer an excellent way to use the energy created by anger.

3. Be patient with yourself.

This is not a single step of growth for most people. It is a journey. However, every journey must begin with a first step. So, begin now to apply the simple insights I have shared with you in this chapter.

Victory over anger is not likely to be won in a single battle. But, when you make the commitment, God will help you win the war. Improvement with effort should encourage you to believe for ultimate success.

4. Thank God for improvement.

Thank God for miracles! Where would we be without them? However, the fact we call them "miracles" identifies them as exceptional and rare. If this was the typical way believers were to manage their emotional problems, such events would be happening far too frequently to call them miracles. So, learn to thank God for improvement.

Paul spells out the process through which healing most often comes in our battle with anger: "Therefore, my dear friends, as you have always obeyed, not only in my presence, but now much more in my absence, continue to work out your salvation with fear and trembling for it is God who works in you to will and to act according to his good pleasure."[13]

Multiply the productivity of your life.

Convert the energy of your angry moments into activities that will bless God and benefit others. Do more than make a friend of your anger—make it your servant. This will help you resolve a major guilt issue in your life.

In the next chapter, you will learn how to tell the

difference between healthy guilt the Holy Spirit raises in your conscience and unhealthy guilt the enemy uses to falsely accuse you.

Discussion Questions

1. How did Jesus' expression of anger in Mark 3:1-6 differ from that of the Pharisees?
2. What guidelines does Ephesians 4:26 give us regarding our expression of anger?
3. For what kind of angry expressions should we feel guilty?
4. How can unrecognized anger be dangerous?
5. Where are some places our anger may be hidden?
6. What are the two extremes we tend to go to in controlling our anger?
7. What are the dangers each poses?
8. How may uncontrolled anger complicate one's life?
9. What are some healthy ways to manage anger?
10. Why is it important to celebrate progress in overcoming destructive expressions of anger?

FOOTNOTES

1 1974 Joint Commission on the Mental Health of Children.
2 Genesis 1:28
3 Psalms 7:11
4 Mark 3:1-6
5 Ephesians 4:26
6 Galatians 2:1-16
7 Acts 15:7 (KJV)
8 Acts 15:6
9 Matthew 7:3-5
10 Goleman, Daniel, **Emotional Intelligence**, New York, N. Y.: Bantam Books, 1997, p. 170
11 Matthew 5:22
12 Matthew 6:9-13
13 Philippians 2:12, 13

CHAPTER SIX

COMING
TO TERMS
WITH
GUILT

After lunch I came back to the office and found a message from a man on the east coast. When I returned his call I found him to be in a lot of emotional pain. You could hear the anxiety in his voice.

Fred was a young man, still in his 20s. After the first few minutes of our conversation I knew the nature of his problem, even though we had not talked before. He was obsessively preoccupied with obscenities directed toward God. He believed these obscenities constituted an unpardonable sin. He saw himself beyond the reach of forgiveness and he couldn't get these thoughts off his mind.

An obsession is like that. It's an idea that persistently intrudes into a person's thought life and preoccupies them. Since he had allowed himself to think these terrible things about God, he believed he was beyond hope. He was doomed to hell.

Over the years I have seen many people with this same obsession. Since it involves obscenities toward God they appear to be spiritual in nature. However, unlike symptoms in a physical illness that usually point to the source of the problem, the purpose of symptoms in emotional disturbances is to distract the person from the real source of his or her emotional pain. Unfortunately, the symptoms usually create more pain and dissipate more energy than would be required to confront the real source of the problem.

Fred's basic problem was emotional, not spiritual.

He was suffering from unhealthy guilt resulting in a need to condemn himself. The punitive mental image of God Fred had formed during his earlier years gave him all the evidence he needed to conclude he had committed the "unpardonable sin." He was convinced he was the world's greatest sinner, a rotten excuse for a human being.

What unresolved problems in a person's past could result in such an exaggerated need for self-condemnation? In most cases with similar symptoms the person is struggling with some kind of unresolved sexual guilt. Such guilt usually stems from histories of masturbation, pornography, premarital sexual contacts, abortion, adultery or bestiality.

Because the symptoms are religious you might think the problem is a spiritual one, but it isn't. The basic problem is rooted in the way they feel and think about themselves.

When you ask people with Fred's problem if they have asked God to forgive them, usually they will give one of two responses. Some will say they have asked God to forgive them many times, but they don't believe He has or will. Others will say they believe God has forgiven them, but they cannot forgive themselves.

In the first instance, the person is responding to his need to condemn himself by harboring a highly punitive view of God. In the second, this need is expressed in his perverse view of himself. In either event, he is fighting a losing battle with unhealthy guilt.

Basically, the problem is more emotional than spiritual. That is, the issue is more within himself than between himself and God.

As you will discover later in the chapter, one of the distinguishing differences between healthy guilt and unhealthy guilt is that unhealthy guilt never yields to forgiveness, regardless of how often one prays for it. But a basic understanding of God's forgiving grace through Jesus Christ tells us that this is a direct contradiction of Scripture.[1]

God never visits unhealthy guilt on anyone.

When a person is afflicted with guilt that confession does not relieve, the guilt is always self-imposed and results in self-condemnation. Then this emotional need to condemn yourself becomes the primary target for spiritual and psychological treatment.

I arranged a series of appointments with Fred. During the first session, when I began to take his sexual history, I discovered what I had first suspected. He was suffering from unresolved masturbatory guilt.

People with obsessions like Fred's are usually unaware that almost a 100 percent of young men and 40 percent or more of young women practice masturbation prior to marriage. So, part of their problem is their tendency to treat this common human experience as though it were some rare evil catastrophe. The commonality of this practice is indicated by studies that found over 93 percent of men and 77 percent of women had varying degrees of experience with masturbation by age 21.[2]

Lust or a matter of private conscience?

Some young people do not feel guilty about masturbation. However, many do. For these, masturbatory guilt poses a major mental health problem. Young people desperately need help in determining whether or not guilt is an appropriate response to this practice, but because the church is so divided over this matter, the clergy offers little or no help. And, very few parents can fill the role as healthy sex educators of their children.

Fred's parents were not only silent about his sexuality while he was growing up they left him feeling that they would be greatly disappointed in him if they were to ever learn that he masturbated. He was simply not to touch himself "down there."

Matters critical to our salvation are thoroughly dealt with in Scripture. However, the practice of masturbation is not specifically mentioned in the Bible. The word does not appear in the Bible.

Therefore, the critical moral issue in masturbation cannot be the activity itself; otherwise, God would have dealt with it directly in Scripture. The moral issue has to do with the nature of a person's fantasies during this activity.

Scripture certainly supports the idea that lustful and pornographic fantasies are sinful. Jesus says: "You have heard that it was said, 'Do not commit adultery.' But I tell you that anyone who looks at a woman lustfully has already committed adultery with her in his heart."[3]

What is lust?

Lust is the selfish use of another person for one's own pleasure. It can involve the persons themselves or pictures, sounds, and stories of people. In any event, lust makes no commitment to another person. A lustful person assumes no responsibility for harmful affects his or her sexual behavior has on another person.

Lust drives people to use or abuse others for their own sexual pleasure. There is no desire for a permanent relationship, but simply a temporary need to use another person's body for selfish sexual gratification.

If this is the nature of a person's fantasy during masturbation and they have a healthy conscience, then guilt is the appropriate response. Anytime fantasies of sexual activities outside the context of marriage are indulged, either before or after marriage, lust is involved. When one uses another person as a temporary fantasy object for sexual gratification they show a total disrespect for that person and divorce the idea of sexual pleasure from marriage in their own mind. Lust says, "I want it now!" Love says, "I can wait."

So, if a person fantasizes about what celebrating sexuality with his or her spouse in marriage will be like while he or she is masturbating and does not feel guilty about the practice, others should not attempt to bring him or her into judgment. When sexual fantasies are not of a specific person and are confined to marriage, I believe the matter of guilt should be left to a person's private con-science. (see Romans 14)

Fantasizing about marriage while you are thinking sexual thoughts and realizing that sexual pleasure with your spouse will be greater than you can experience alone is a healthy way to manage your sexuality before mar-riage. Keeping your sexual fantasies true to the person you will meet and marry years before you know who he or she is will give you the sexual discipline to be true to him or her once you are married.

Because you are never "as good as married" until you are married, your sexual fantasies are healthier if they remain focused on the idea of being married. Holding your future partner at this level of respect until you are married can only add to the fulfillment of your marital experience.

Is forgiveness based on our promise to quit?

Fred was convinced he was hopelessly doomed because he had lied to God so many times about quitting this practice. Most of those who live under the weight of unresolved masturbatory guilt have been taught that unless they promise God to quit masturbating He will not forgive them.

So they promise God that if He will forgive them they will not do it again. He forgives them, but after a few days they do it again. Now, they feel they must persuade

God that they are all the more serious about their determination to quit. On this basis, they desperately plea for His additional forgiveness. Then, they do it again. Eventually, since they do not quit they assume that God withdraws His forgiveness. Then they live with this accumulation of unresolved sexual guilt convincing them their sin is unpardonable.

Is this the way God deals with us about other sins? If so, we are all in trouble. Who among us has quit everything for which we have been forgiven?

Only God knows how many times you and I have had to be forgiven for the same sin before we finally grew out of it. And, we are currently battling many others for which we still need his grace. If God does not deal with us this way about our other sins, why should a special case be made of masturbation?

This approach is unsound theologically because it bases forgiveness on our ability to stop some practice for which we feel guilty. If this is true then salvation is by our works, not by God's grace. God never forgives us on the basis of any promise we make to Him. He forgives us because of what Christ did for us at Calvary. This is what grace is all about.[4]

Teaching children that God only forgives those sins we quit is also unsound psychologically, because it creates an obsessive need to remember what it is we are not supposed to do. This keeps the subject on our mind. Our preoccupation with it makes it more likely we will do it again. The continuation of this cycle feeds our obsession with the thought and our bondage to the habit.

As I explained this to Fred, you could hear the relief in his voice. As you might imagine, this was the first time in his life anyone had ever discussed this subject with him. Simply discovering that others had similar struggles helped him not to feel so odd about himself.

"What should I do when I do it again?" he asked. "Well," I said, "what do you do when you say things again that you promised God you wouldn't say anymore?" "I ask God to forgive me," Fred replied. "And you believe that He does," I reflected. "Sure," he confidently responded. How long have you been managing your verbal sins this way?" I asked. "Ever since I've been a Christian," he answered. "Why haven't you quit saying things you shouldn't?" I challenged. "I want to," he insisted. "I try." "So, even though you haven't quit, God still forgives you as often as you ask Him because He knows you want to quit and you try. Do you suppose God would treat your problem with masturbation the same way?" I asked. "I never thought of it that way before," Fred said reflectively. "I believe He would." "So do I," I reassured him.

This became the basis of our treatment approach. Fred began to see that God was not condemning him. He was condemning himself. As he learned to bring this part of his life under the atonement, unhealthy guilt diminished. His preoccupation with obscenities toward God gradually disappeared. Today, he is married and enjoying an active place of Christian service in his local church.

Man's struggle with guilt runs throughout Scripture.
There was Adam and Eve hiding from God in the garden of Eden, Cain trying to explain Abel's death to God, Noah getting drunk and naked, Abraham casting Hagar and Ishmael out of his home, Jacob wrestling all night with an angel fearful his brother would kill him, Joseph's brothers groveling before him as prime minister of Egypt, Moses burying the Egyptian he slew, Achan stashing the Babylonian garment in his tent, Samson waking in Delilah's lap with his hair cut and his power gone, David hearing Nathan's parable, the adulterous woman

bring thrown down at Jesus feet, Judas bargaining for 30 pieces of silver, Peter denying his Lord. This is just a short list of Bible characters who felt the pangs of the human family's common struggle with guilt.

And you and I join this pathetic parade when we displease God, disappoint our family, or deny our better selves. The violation of these relationships is the most common source of healthy guilt.

Healthy guilt builds good character.

The pain of healthy guilt is God's way of calling our attention to boundaries that have been violated. We've said things that have harmed others. We've done things that offended our relationships. God wants us to see that our relationships are healed and these boundaries restored. These boundaries are defined and reinforced by your conscience.

Paul frequently addresses the subject of conscience. He tells Timothy about two men who made shipwreck of their faith because they failed to listen to their conscience. Then, he urges Timothy to hold onto his good conscience.[5]

The ability to respond to healthy guilt feelings is essential to building our character. By coming to terms with these feelings honestly and resolving them in ways that restore others trust in us we demonstrate good character.

Over time, a person's character is revealed by his or her attitudes and behavior. Once you know the person's character, you can predict fairly accurately how that person will respond to different situations. Character is both observable and predictable.

People can act out of character.

Of course, once in a while, any of us can and will

act out of character. That is, a person of bad character is capable of doing some good things. A habitual thief and liar may help an elderly person home with groceries, but that doesn't make the thief a person of good character.

On the other hand, once in a while, a person of good character may do some bad things. For example, someone whose character has been above reproach for years may misbehave over a brief period of time, but that doesn't necessarily change their basic character. This is difficult for some Christians to accept, either about themselves or others.

One of the tragedies of the church is that when good people have momentary lapses of character, the many faithful years they have invested in God's kingdom are so easily forgotten. There is a tendency to judge them harshly for behavior which is basically out of character for them.

Perhaps this is why Paul admonishes us, "Brothers, if someone is caught in a sin, you who are spiritual should restore him gently. But watch yourself, or you also may be tempted."[6]

The power of your conscience

It is your conscience that makes your character so predictable. Your character is a product of your conscience. The Bible emphasizes the relationship between conscience and character. Paul says, "The Spirit clearly says that in latter times some will abandon the faith and follow deceiving spirits and things taught by demons. Such teachings come through hypocritical liars, whose consciences have been seared as with a hot iron."[7]

Where does your conscience come from?

God has given the capacity for conscience to everyone. The Scriptures make this very clear: "Indeed, when

Gentiles who do not have the law, do by nature things required by the law, they are a law for themselves, even though they do not have the law, since they show that the requirements of the law are written on their hearts, their consciences also bearing witness, and their thoughts now accusing, now even defending them."[8]

Our conscience is a divine mark which sets us off from brute beasts. Every normal person is born with the capacity for conscience, but the content of our conscience is culturally derived. What each of us feels guilty for is greatly affected by the part of the world in which we were born and the part of that country in which we were raised.

For example, Americans eat beef, but those who live in Hindu countries would consider this to be a sacrilege. On the other hand, they might eat dog, which we would find most repulsive. Your conscience is also affected by the particular part of the country in which you were raised. For example, children in the South where I was raised were taught to address adults respectfully: "Yes, ma'am." "No, ma'am." "Yes, sir." "No, sir." These courtesies were ingrained in my conscience as a child, but I soon discovered they didn't exist in children raised in Ohio where we moved when I was 13.

Who forms your conscience?

Your family forms your conscience. This is why Adam could have a son in his own likeness.[9] The two processes that make this possible are genetic transmission and the psychological dynamics involved in conscience formation. Genes pass on to us the physical and emotional characteristics of our parents and conscience transmits to us the family character. Far more important than the physical characteristics we receive from our parents is the spiritual heritage they transmit to us. This does not mean that being born to parents of good character guarantees you a good character anymore than being born to parents of bad character automatically dooms you to be a person of bad character.

The formation of your own character grows out of the complex interaction between and among you, your parents, and your siblings. Some children rebel against the godly character of their parents. Other children determine to reject the bad character of their parents. Parents should never be blamed for nor take the credit for the character of their child. Ezekiel settled this issue for us centuries ago.[10]

Three qualities of a good conscience

One of the most valuable gifts we can receive from our parents and others who impact our lives is a good conscience. What is a good conscience? Here are three qualities of a good conscience.

First, a good conscience is neither too broad nor too narrow. It won't let you get away with too much, but it won't condemn you for too little. A good conscience will not let you be comfortable in breaking the law, or offending the important relationships in your life.

Second, a good conscience is consistent in its vigilance. It grants its approval and imposes its sanctions regardless of time or place. It will not be conveniently silenced!

Third, a good conscience is forgiving. Once you respond to the pangs of a good conscience with confession and, if necessary, some form of restitution, it won't torment you any longer. It will let you be at peace with God and yourself.

How is our conscience formed?

Our conscience develops out of our interaction with our parents during the first five years of life. It emerges gradually as parental love selectively alleviates infant fears. Initially, this interaction between parent and child centers largely in the amount of physical space given to us as infants.

Your brain consistently associates pain and pleasure with person and place. Any pediatrician will verify this observation. They have done everything possible to make children less apprehensive in their office. For example, they no longer wear a white coat to identify them as a source of pain. Their office no longer smells like medicine. They have surrendered their hypodermic syringes to nurses. They provide little gifts for their patients. But, as long as our infants get their immunization shots in that office, we can expect them to scream out their predictable protests as soon as they enter. Regardless of what is done to neutralize that place, their brain tells them that sooner or later they are going to get it "in the end."

Your child's brain associates pain and pleasure with the emotions of fear and love. We fear the places where we experience pain and we are fond of the places where we experience pleasure. This simple mechanism becomes the cradle of conscience.

You can give your child a healthy conscience.

By avoiding certain definable extremes and following a very simple three-step formula, you can be sure you are giving your child a healthy conscience. Let's look first at the extremes to be avoided.

Be sure the limits you set for your child are not too broad. Allowing a child to jump up and down on the furniture and to talk disrespectfully to adults is not in the child's best interests. Giving too much physical and emotional freedom produces a child other people can't stand. Later in life, such broad limits for the conscience leaves the child without the protection of painful prodding when values and ideals are about to be violated.

On the other hand, avoid setting limits for your child that are too narrow. This results in your child seeing you as being very difficult if not impossible to please. Often, being continually confronted with such narrow limits produces a guilt-prone child who is displeased with himself much of the time.

Inconsistent limits are the most devastating. When parents change limits at unpredictable times and in unpredictable ways the child becomes unsure about what is expected of him and insecure in his parent's love. Consistent limits are essential to a healthy conscience and a good character.

You create a healthy conscience in your child when you follow this simple formula:

Be Fair.

How can you know when your limits are fair? Simply put yourself in your child's place. Then ask yourself how much liberty you could safely manage at that age. Such an application of Christian compassion toward your children is one of the most practical ways I know to test the fairness of your limits.

Be Firm.

If your limits are fair, then why not make them firm. Firm limits that are fair produce a sense of loving security in your child. Part of our fallen nature drives us to test—and protest any limits put on our behavior. So, don't depend upon your child's pleasant acceptance of your limits to indicate their appropriateness. Remember how vigorously you protested limits your parents set for you as a child. Any healthy person must learn to live within limits. The sooner in life we discover that, the better.

Be Friendly.

Unfortunately, some parents only know how to be firm when they are angry. Without knowing it, they are teaching their children to delay compliance with their limits until the parent's voice reaches a certain decibel level reflecting the unmistakable sound of anger. "How many times have I told you? The answer is, 'No.' Don't you understand that? It's spelled n-o. 'No!'"

This kind of harangue is not necessary. Remember what Paul says: "Fathers, do not embitter your children, or they will become discouraged."[11]

Gently, but firmly, enforce your limits. "I'm sorry you feel so angry because I said you couldn't go. But my job is to set limits for you. Your job is to come to terms with them. All your crying and whining isn't going to change what I've decided, so you may as well get busy doing something that will take your mind off this." Such a response establishes the parent's control, but it also helps the youngster learn how to accept limits without being too preoccupied by his frustration.

How healthy is your conscience?

As a parent, how healthy is your conscience? What are the things that make you feel guilty? A healthy conscience will impose guilt when you are engaging in behavior which endangers your life, your character, your property, or the life, character, or property of someone else.

Once conscience is formed, it is highly resistant to change. For most of us, that is a blessing. We have had loving parents who have given us a healthy conscience. Even after we have established our own personal faith in Christ we do not have to struggle with a faulty conscience.

After we become Christians our conscience has to be retrained by the Scriptures so we can become sensitive to the limits placed on our behavior by the Bible. When this has been done, our transformed conscience continues to be a consistent monitor of our behavior—rewarding us when we obey Christ's teaching and reprimanding us when we disobey. A healthy conscience plays a prominent role in determining the extent to which Christ is reflected in our attitudes and behavior.

How to treat a sick conscience

The resistance of the conscience to change presents some Christians with an urgent need for spiritual healing. Their conscience is unhealthy. Thank God, the Scripture makes provision for this change. *"Do not conform any longer to the pattern of this world, but be transformed by the renewing of your mind. Then you will be able to test and approve what God's will is—his good, pleasing and perfect will."*[12]

How do you know if you need healing for your conscience? Look carefully at the role guilt has played in your past. If you seldom feel guilty or are crippled by guilt your conscience needs divine attention. Here are some A-B-C's to help you facilitate any needed change.

"A" - Acknowledge your need for healing.

Some have become Christians because of crises created by habits, attitudes, and behaviors which have demonstrated a callous disregard of others in their own selfish pursuit of pleasure. All of this has precipitated little, if any, guilt in them.

These people need to learn how to discipline themselves. Their attitudes and behavior contradict the Scriptures and bring unnecessary pain into the lives of others. Their consciences need to be narrowed and strengthened.

Among our treatment population we are more likely to find Christians who are suffering from a conscience which is too narrow. That is why I have chosen to give this problem special attention later in the chapter.

"B" - Believe God can help you.

If God can bring you into His family through a "new birth," then He can heal your sick conscience. The Bible provides us with beautiful examples of this. Look at Jacob. His conscience was too broad. He bought his brother's birthright and stole his brother's blessing without feeling enough guilt to see how wrong this was.

So, God planned an all-night wrestling match between Jacob and the angel of the Lord. This spiritual battle brought healing to Jacob's conscience. From that time on Jacob experienced too much emotional pain to continue his devious ways.[13]

Then, there was Mary Magdalene. Before she met Jesus, there is no indication that she suffered guilt for earning her living as a prostitute. However, when she came to Christ He healed her conscience and changed her character.[14]

Also, Paul underwent a real transformation of conscience when he became a Christian. Up until that time, he was driven by a Pharisaical conscience. He was the biggest legalist of the legalists.[15]

Can you imagine what a harsh, judgmental conscience Saul of Tarsus must have had before Christ touched him? Yet, after his conversion a miracle of inner healing took place in Paul's life that gave him the flexibility to "become all things to all men so that by all possible means I might save some."

How did such a psychological miracle happen? Jesus not only transformed Paul's life but He and also healed his conscience.

"C" - Concentrate your efforts on the correction you need to make in your conscience.

Correction of your conscience is part of your sanctification or healing that begins to take place when you accept Christ into your life. Even though a major adjustment of conscience may take place miraculously at conversion, refinements usually follow throughout one's Christian life. Remember, your spiritual life will only be as healthy as your conscience. So, keep working at it!

Healthy vs. unhealthy guilt

The person whose conscience is too narrow and rigid will have the greatest struggle in this battle for a healthy conscience. Often, such a person is afraid that if he doesn't feel guilty about every little thing he does wrong he may not make it to heaven. His conscience is a tyrant. He suffers from unhealthy guilt.

What is the difference between healthy and unhealthy guilt? Let's take a look at three characteristics that make this distinction for us:

1. Unhealthy guilt has its roots in rules, healthy guilt in relationships.

I grew up around a religion of rules. Unfortunately, more attention was focused on breaking the rules than on the violation of relationships.

It was against the rules to play on Sunday. Even during the week we couldn't play the Old Maid card game unless we pulled the drapes to be sure we wouldn't be a stumbling block to someone who might look through the windows and think we were playing "cards." I was afraid to play pinball machines because if Christ were to return or if I should die before I had a chance to repent, my salvation could be in jeopardy.

The Christians in Galatia were prone to this kind of

legalism. Even though Paul brought them out from such bondage, persuasive teachers attempted to put them under the bondage of the law again.[16] Such legalistic faith tends to make critical judges out of believers. They become more concerned about keeping religious rules than nurturing the significant relationships in their lives.

Healthy guilt inflicts enough pain to warn you that important relationships in your life are being threatened by your attitudes and behavior. Take time to survey the important relationships in your life. How healthy are they? What is the state of your relationship with God? How much of yourself have you invested in the interest of healthy family relationships? Who are your closest friends? Are you caring for those relationships?

These are the vital issues of your life. A healthy conscience will force you to face them honestly. A good conscience will inflict enough emotional pain on you to bring these matters to your attention. When you address them responsibly, a healthy conscience will not only reward you with relief, but will also give you the kind of commendation that leaves you feeling good about the priorities of your life.

2. Both healthy and unhealthy guilt carry with them a compulsion to confess.

The key to distinguishing the difference between healthy and unhealthy guilt is in the kinds of things you are being driven to confess. Honestly ask yourself whether the issues being raised by your conscience are vital to a healthy relationship with God and the people who are important to you.

Remember, Jesus identified the conscience of the Pharisees as unhealthy because they could not distinguish the difference between rules and relationships. Or, as He put it, they couldn't tell the difference between: a "speck of sawdust" and a "plank; "gnats and camels;" or, the inside and outside of a cup or dish.[17]

3. Unhealthy guilt never yields to forgiveness, but healthy guilt always does.

I often ask people suffering from unhealthy guilt, "What is it that you've done to prompt this awful, unrelenting guilt?" The most common response is, "I don't know." As soon as someone tells me this I know their guilt is not from God. If God is the source of our guilt He always lets us know exactly why He is making us feel guilty. You and I may hold things against each other without revealing what it is, but God is not like that.

Husbands and wives sometimes play these games with each other. It is common for a couple to head home from some social gathering with the wife seated so far from her husband that if it weren't for the door she would be outside the car.

He inquires, "What's wrong, Honey? What did I do? What did I say? Why are you so upset?" Obviously pouting, she folds her arms and disgustingly responds, "If you don't know, I'm not going to tell you!"

Husbands are just as capable of playing this game. In a similar situation the man may back out of the drive like a maniac, peel rubber as he heads for home, and fill the car with angry stony silence. His wife, attempting to relieve the situation, may say, "I know I must have done something wrong. What did I do? What did I say? What's wrong?" The man's thundering response is likely to be, "You know what's wrong!"

People suffering from unhealthy guilt think God is like that. They think they have to beg God to tell them the source of their guilt. Nothing could be farther from the truth! If the guilt you experience is from God, He will be specific in identifying the source as soon as you ask Him.

God does not play games with us. The only reason the Holy Spirit ever inflicts guilt on us is to safeguard our relationship with God and the important people in our lives. The purpose of divine conviction is to bring you to confession and forgiveness.

As soon as we change the attitudes and behavior that threaten the important relationships in our life, God will remove the pain. Remember what the Scriptures say! "If we confess our sins, he is faithful and just and will forgive us our sins, and purify us from all unrighteousness."[18] Guilt that remains after you've honestly confessed your sins to God is unhealthy—the work of a sick conscience.

It is tragic to see people punishing themselves for mistakes of their past. They seem to believe that their willingness to suffer somehow impresses God with the sincerity of their remorse. Jesus died for our sins, and to suggest that any pain I inflict upon myself could add to the atonement purchased for me by His death is sacrilege.

The idol of "the me that might have been!"

When Evelyn first came to see me she was in her 40's. She was anxious, angry, and guilty. Evelyn had been on tranquilizers for years.

After each of her first few sessions she would say, "I know there's something I have to tell you, if I am going to get better, but I just don't have the courage. I'm afraid you'll lose all respect for me once you know."

I reassured her that it was highly unlikely she would tell me anything I hadn't heard many times before. Her secret had accumulated so much anxiety through the years that she simply could not bear facing it.

Finally, she opened a session by announcing, "This is the day. I made up my mind to get this whole business out of me today." So, this was her story. When Evelyn was a teenager, she became sexually involved with a young

man from her church. Unfortunately, she conceived.
When it became obvious that she was pregnant, the pastor
forced her and the young man to get up in front of a
crowded sanctuary on Sunday morning and confess that
they had sinned. (By that time what they had done was
apparent to everyone.)

In spite of this humiliation, Evelyn and her
boyfriend stayed in the church. They married and with the
help of their families began to build a stable marriage. To
spare Margie, their first child, the embarrassment of discovering she was conceived before her parents were married, they managed to have the date on her birth certificate
changed.

Through the years, Evelyn and her husband
became respected members of the community and leaders
in their church. However, Evelyn's sick conscience continued to inflict pain on her over this unfortunate mistake
of her youth.

Her best friend in whom she had confided during
the trying weeks of her first pregnancy, moved away short-
ly after Margie was born. A few months before Evelyn
came to see me, this woman's husband was transferred
back into the area. Evelyn's youngest daughter, Becky,
and her friend's youngest daughter had developed a close
relationship.

Evelyn's big fear was that this woman would feel a
moral obligation to tell Becky the story of Margie's conception. There were moments when Evelyn knew her
friend would never do this. However, much of the time
she was tormented with this fear.

Once Evelyn had told me this whole story, I said,
"Is that all?" She cried, "Is that all? Isn't that enough?"

I assured her, "Evelyn, I've heard that story many,
many times. Did you ask the Lord to forgive you at the
time?" "Oh," she sobbed, "I asked God to forgive me then,

and I've asked Him a 100 times or more since then."

"Do you believe He has forgiven you?" I asked.

"Oh, sure, I believe God has forgiven me, but how can I forgive myself?"

As I became aware of the tremendous toll this unhealthy guilt had extracted from Evelyn's life, the thought made me angry. Just as Jesus said, Satan the thief, had stolen years of emotional peace from this child of God.[19] I felt the anger in my voice as I said, "Oh! The blood of Jesus was adequate to satisfy the holy nature of God, but it's not good enough for 'your holy conscience.' Is that what you are telling me? Must God send another Son to die for 'your holy conscience?' Isn't one Calvary enough?"

By this time Evelyn was sobbing uncontrollably. I heard her say through tears, "My God, I've never seen it like that before." It suddenly dawned on her that uncon-sciously, she had been trying to suffer for her own sins. She had forgotten what Isaiah said, "He was pierced for our transgressions, he was crushed for our iniquities; the punishment that brought us peace was upon him, and by his wounds we are healed."[20]

God healed Evelyn that day. Upon her next visit her medical doctor began to withdraw her from the tran-quilizers she had been on for years. I saw her for follow-up visits at three- and six-month intervals. She remained healthy and happy!

The healing that came to her that day could have been hers years before. After all, the guilt she had need-lessly inflicted upon herself was borne by Christ for all of us.

There's something enigmatic about a person like Evelyn being unable to forgive herself. Usually, such per-sons are the last ones in the world to think of themselves as idolaters. Yet, they are worshiping an idol. How many times do you suppose such people have said to themselves: "Oh, if only it hadn't happened that way. How different my life might have been. But now it can never be what it might have been. My whole life is ruined."

Unconsciously, these people are worshiping the idol of the "me-that-might-have-been." Because the "me-that-might-have-been" can never be, they refuse to accept the "me-that-is." And because they won't accept the "me-that-is," they can't discover the "me-that-can-be" in Jesus.

That kind of attitude toward life is like a little girl who has dropped her china doll and broken it. Her mother may pick it up and carefully mend it, but the little girl refuses to take it back because she knows it has cracks in it. Instead of focusing on the fact that she has her doll back, she keeps her eyes glued on the cracks. Her doll is her idol.

When you won't forgive yourself of some mistakes in your past, you're making an idol out of the "me-that-might-have-been." If you will smash that idol, and forgive yourself, God will help you discover the "me-that-can-be" in Jesus. Only by letting go of the past will you reach the future that can be yours.

Some people find this such a battle that they spend much of their life depressed. This kind of situational depression is very different from biochemical depression. In the next chapter I will give you some ways to tell them apart and I will share some suggestions for dealing with depression.

Discussion Questions

1. What are three characteristics of a healthy conscience?
2. Where does one's conscience come from?
3. When and how is conscience formed?
4. What are the differences in punishment and discipline?
5. Is it possible to have one without the other?
6. What are the three F's of good discipline?
7. How can a person's conscience be changed?
8. What is the A-B-C method for changing an unhealthy conscience?
9. What are the three characteristics of healthy guilt?
10. What are the three characteristics of unhealthy guilt?

FOOTNOTES

[1] I John 1:9
[2] Janus, Samuel and Cynthia, The Janus Report, New York, NY: John Wiley and Sons, Inc., pp75-79.
[3] Matthew 5:27, 28
[4] Ephesians 2:8, 9
[5] I Timothy 1:18-20
[6] Galatians 6:1
[7] I Timothy 4:1, 2
[8] Romans 12:14
[9] Genesis 5:3
[10] Ezekiel 18:1-32
[11] Colossians 3:21
[12] Romans 12:2
[13] Philippians 3:4-6
[14] I Corinthians 9:19-22
[15] Galatians 1:13,14
[16] Galatians 3:1-3
[17] Matthew 7:3; 23:23-28
[18] I John 1:9
[19] John 10:10
[20] Isaiah 53:5

CHAPTER SEVEN

DEALING
WITH
DEPRESSION

Whenever I help a person deal with depression I'm reminded of the struggle my first wife had with this emotional nightmare. She battled depression most of her life, but it almost killed her when we were expecting our first child.

Toxemia plagued her pregnancy from the third month and finally forced her to give Caesarian birth to our son eight months after he was conceived. I will never forget the haunting scene in the ambulance on our way home from the hospital. Out of the blue a frightening ghastly expression came across her gaunt little face as she announced to me, "I'm just like Judas. There is no hope for me. I've committed the unpardonable sin. You and Billy will be better off without me."

I tried to assure her that we both desperately needed her, but nothing I said seemed to penetrate the dark cloud that had suddenly taken over her mind.

Over the next several weeks we would have similar conversations again and again. None helped. I couldn't understand what had happened to my wife and neither could she.

Even during those dark days, her consistent daily devotional life told me that she dearly loved the Lord. And there was no doubt in my mind about His love for her. Yet later she would recall this as a time in her life when she had no conscious awareness of God's love for her or even His presence. Her battle with depression left her feeling as though God had totally forsaken her.

For six months it was as though she were being stalked by some merciless specter of death. On three different occasions she tried to take her life. For several months after her last suicide attempt she was still walking through a world of deep valleys and dark skies. There is no way to describe the powerlessness and helplessness I felt during that time.

Even though she couldn't believe in her recovery, I never allowed myself to doubt it. I sought every way humanly possible to help her. Nothing worked. However, I did learn the importance of allowing her to express her feelings to me.

I never will forget how her battle with this beast came to an end. We were holding evangelistic meetings in Beckley, West Virginia. The pastor and his wife had gone to make hospital calls. My wife and I took advantage of this private time to have our devotions. That morning, while we were kneeling in prayer, she experienced the consciousness of God's presence. This was the first time in six months she had been free from that horrifying feeling of being totally abandoned by Him.

There was nothing special about that morning to indicate what was about to happen. I had always believed that she would get better. In my heart, I knew that she would be aware of God's presence again some day. However, I had no evidence that it would happen that morning.

But it did! God broke through those heavy black clouds of depression and lifted her out of her despondency into His presence. This became obvious to me when she rose from her knees and came over to embrace me. There was energy in her face, a gleam in her eye, and an excitement in her voice that seemed almost too good to be true. She said, "Honey, the Lord touched me this morning, and I feel so much better."

What a celebration we had! It would be several months before depression would be an uncommon thing in her day, but the back of the beast was broken that morning.

The unforgettable pain of that experience has given me a deep compassion for people who suffer from depression. Today, almost 19 million American adults do battle with this devilish dragon each year.[1]

The "Age of Depression"

The increasing frequency with which this mental agony grips the people of our nation suggests that we are living in the "Age of Depression." Each successive generation of Americans born since the beginning of the 20th century has shown higher rates of major depression and lower ages of onset. Today, young people in their teens and 20s are at least three times more likely to suffer from major depression than their grandparents were 50 years ago. This increased level of depression among the young is reflected by the fact that suicide has become the second highest cause of death among teenagers. It only follows automobile accidents, and there is no way of knowing how many of these may be disguised suicides. As strange as it may seem, the old in our society are at much lower risk for depression than are the young.[2]

When asked to speculate as to why there is this rising trend of depression among our children and youth, Dr. Frederick Goodman, former director of the National Institute of Mental Health, had this to say, "There's been a tremendous erosion of the nuclear family—a doubling of the divorce rate, a drop in parents time available to children, and an increase in mobility. You don't grow up knowing your extended family much anymore. The losses of these stable sources of self-identification means a greater susceptibility to depression."[3]

Psychologist Martin Seligman from the University of Pennsylvania adds, "For the last thirty or forty years we've seen the ascendance of individualism and a waning of larger beliefs in religion and in supports from the community and extended family. That means a loss of resources that can buffet you against setbacks and failures. To the extent you see a failure as something that is lasting and which you magnify to taint everything in your life, you are prone to let a momentary defeat become a lasting source of hopelessness. But if you have a larger perspective, like a belief in God and an afterlife, and you lose your job, it is just a momentary defeat." [4]

Others agree that societal changes such as: the institutionalization of infant and child care, increase in divorce, single parent families, and step families have created an environment for our children and youth that substantially increases the risk of depression for them.[5] Tom Brokaw's observation while commenting on one of his World War II families, illustrates this point well: ". . . they did keep their faith in God, in each other, and in the belief that life is about helping others. They passed that along to their two daughters and their surviving son. That's another legacy of the World War II generation, the strong commitment to family values and community. They were mature beyond their years, in their twenties, and when they married and began families it was not a matter of thinking 'Well, let's see how this works out . . .'".[6]

You and I are challenged to live in this toxic social environment that so readily breeds depression. Therefore I hope you will find the information about depression and the suggestions for dealing with it practical and helpful.

Our focus will be on these four frequently-asked questions: "What is depression?" "What are its symptoms?" "Who suffers from it?" "How can a person deal with it?"

What is depression?

As a form of human suffering, depression has been around for a long time. It is probably as old as the human race. Depression is the most common form of emotional pain that is commonly identified as an emotional state of dejection and sadness. It can range from mild discouragement and downheartedness to feelings of utter hopelessness and despair.

In the fourth century B.C., Hippocrates, the father of modern medicine, gave us our first clinical definition of depression. He identified it as the "black humor" which he called "melancholia."

The National Institute of Mental Health defines a depressive disorder as, "an illness that involves the body, mood and thoughts. It affects the way a person eats and sleeps, the way one feels about oneself and the way one thinks about things. It is not the same as a passing blue mood. It is not a sign of personal weakness or a condition that can be willed or wished away. People with a depressive illness cannot merely 'pull themselves together' and get better. Without treatment symptoms can last for weeks, months, or years."[7]

Of course, people who have experienced depression are the real experts in describing what it is like. Theirs is a far more realistic understanding of depression although it is difficult to put into words. For example, in a fit of depression Abraham Lincoln wrote, "If what I feel were equally distributed to the whole human family, there would not be one cheerful face on earth."[8]

One out of every four adult women and one out of every six adult men will suffer a major depressive episode sometime in their lives. Fifty to 75 percent of these will have a second episode during their lifetime.

Depression extracts a devastating economic toll from this nation. Estimates for the national costs of depression range from 30 to 40 billion dollars a year. This does not include the 200 million days of work that are lost each year in the United States because of depression.[9]

What are the symptoms of depression?

The symptoms of depression will vary with its intensity. From time to time most of us will experience the "blues." The zest goes out of life. We feel sad and dejected. We may retreat into temporary silence or reflect a surly or melancholic mood.

However, these normal "downs" of life last only a day or two. As a rule of thumb, if your depression doesn't last longer than four days just consider it a normal bout with the "blues." When it lasts a week or longer you should bring it to the attention of a competent health professional.

As your depression deepens a cluster of the following symptoms will be present:

- Persistent sad, anxious or empty mood
- Feelings of hopelessness and pessimism
- Feelings of guilt, worthlessness and helplessness
- Loss of interest or pleasure in hobbies and activities that were once enjoyed, including sex
- Decreased energy, fatigue, being "slowed down"
- Difficulty concentrating, remembering, making decisions
- Insomnia, early-morning awakening, or oversleeping
- Appetite and/or weight loss or overeating and weight gain
- Thoughts of death or suicide, suicide attempts
- Restlessness, irritability[10]

Usually, depression comes from the painful circumstances of one's life. However, at times, it is brought on by disturbed neurochemistry. If this is the source of your depression you are likely to experience some of these unique symptoms:

1. Pervasive anhedonia or a total absence of pleasure

Unlike the person whose depression grows out of a crisis or overwhelming circumstances, nothing can brighten your mood. Hearing that a loved one was healed from a crippling disease will bring you no joy. Learning that you have suddenly become wealthy will not bring a smile to your face. Your sense of humor is gone. You are incapable of pleasure.

2. An unresponsive mood

A normal person reacts emotionally to the mood of the group he or she is with at the time. Even a person who is depressed because of their circumstances can be cheered up temporarily by the people around him. However, if you are neurochemically depressed person you will remain impassive and oblivious to the mood of your social environment.

3. Sudden onset

If you are neurochemically depressed the onset of your depression is likely to be sudden and unrelated to the ongoing circumstances in your life. When you ask people suffering from this kind of depression how they became aware of their depression they often say things like, "One afternoon while I was at work it just felt like a dark cloud came over my mind." Or, "It was like being in a bright room and having someone pull the shades down."

The biggest concern is suicide.

Regardless of the source of the depression, the most serious symptom is the presence of suicidal thoughts. Contrary to popular opinion, people who commit suicide do talk about it. In fact, only rarely does a person commit suicide without giving some indication of his or her intentions. If you find yourself preoccupied with suicidal thoughts reach out to your family for help; or better yet, go to the emergency room of your local hospital. The safest thing you can do is to have a mental health professional who is qualified assess your risk of suicide.

If your loved one needs to be hospitalized for their protection and they won't consent to it, then take whatever legal steps may be required to give them the protection they need. It is better to tolerate their protests than live with the regret of any negligence on your part.

I have never known depression to kill anyone. If the depressed person can be given the protection he or she needs during the most despairing time of his or her illness he or she will survive. Although it is difficult to protect a person who frequently thinks of suicide, as a family member you want to be sure you have taken every step you can to prevent it.

Who suffers from depression?

Among church people there seems to be a widespread, but mistaken notion that if a person is a Christian he will be protected from emotional problems of any kind. However, everybody is subject to mental health problems and most of us will have our bouts with them at some point in life. If you haven't had any, be grateful!

A careful study of both the Old and New testaments clearly indicate that throughout the ages prominent Bible characters suffered from depression.

Job suffered from major depression. Tornadoes had

blown down his buildings and killed his children. Thieves had stolen his herds. His health was gone. He was a mass of sores from his head to his feet. Job had lost everything! Neither his wife nor his friends would give him any comfort in his agony.

Silenced for seven days by his losses, Job sat with his friends.[11] Can you imagine being so depressed that you would sit for seven days without uttering a word?

When Job finally opened his mouth he cursed the day of his birth: *"May the day of my birth perish, and the night it was said, 'A boy is born!' That day—may it turn to darkness; may God above not care about it; may no light shine upon it . . . Why did I not perish at birth, and die as I came from the womb?"*[12] His wife, not knowing how else to comfort him, advised him to, "Curse God and die!"[13] And, remember, God told Satan that Job was the best man in the world.[14]

Even a casual reading of the 42nd Psalm tells you David was depressed. Listen to what he said: *"My tears have been my food day and night, while men say to me all day long, "Where is your God?"*[15]

From every indication, Elijah suffered from a bi-polar disorder. There was no doubt about the power he had with God. He had called fire down from heaven on one occasion and rain on another. He had slaughtered the prophets of Baal by the hundreds. Yet right in the middle of this spiritual high, depression struck him. After fleeing from Jezebel who had sworn to kill him, he found himself sitting under a juniper tree bemoaning his fate and wishing he were dead. He prayed, *"I have had enough, LORD. Take my life; I am no better than my ancestors."*[16]

Notice how irrational this prayer was. If Elijah had really wanted to die why didn't he let Jezebel kill him? She would have been delighted to answer this prayer for him, and he could have saved himself such an exhausting flight.

When the crowing of the cock reminded Peter that he had betrayed his Lord just as Jesus predicted he would, Peter ". . . *went out and wept bitterly.*"[17] The next few days were days of deep depression for this repentant apostle.

If some of the best and most spiritual people in the Bible got depressed, you and I certainly should not allow guilt to compound our misery when we are depressed.

Can anyone suffer from depression?

Unfortunately, when we get depressed there still seem to be some in the church who think we must have some dark and hidden sin in our lives for which we need to repent. I remember the unnecessary pain this caused my wife and me while we were going through her difficult postpartum depression. I say "we" because, when your mate is seriously depressed you are also deeply affected by it.

Unfortunately, at the time, we couldn't find a pastor who understood our mental health problem. And, we couldn't find a mental health professional who respected our faith. Our minister friends advised me, "You just need to get her more into the Word and prayer." Mental health professionals would say, "It's your religion. That's what's making your wife mentally ill. Just look at her symptoms. She believes she has committed some unpardonable sin. Get her out of her crazy religion and she will be all right."

I knew my wife was not suffering from depression because she neglected Scripture reading and prayer. She was spending much more time reading the Bible and praying than me, and I wasn't depressed. And, I knew that her faith was a too important part of her life for her to be helped by abandoning it. She needed the support of a healthy faith and competent mental health care.

Some people are still at the mercy of such unnecessarily narrow points of view from their church and their physician. More and more mental health professionals, however, are becoming aware that a healthy faith can alleviate many of the anxieties and tensions of people with emotional problems. And more pastors are beginning to understand that many Christians can benefit from medication and the competent care of mental health professionals who respect their faith.

As you can see, anyone can suffer from depression and, at some time in life, most people do. No depth of spirituality or degree of perfection makes us immune. So we should never allow our need for professional help in dealing with depression to reflect negatively on our relationship with God. If we need medication for depression, we should take it without feeling guilty or embarrassed. After all, when our heart, kidneys, or lungs need medication we take it. Why should we discriminate against our brain if it needs medical help?

What causes depression?

Depression is often a secondary symptom of physical illness. This is why a competent professional person will want you to have a physical examination before assuming that your depression is psychologically induced. Often, the successful treatment of your physical problem remedies your depression.

Also depression can come from painful circumstances in your life: marital tension, personal illness, parent-child conflict, work aggravations, business reverses, boredom, frustration with friends, or parental insensitivity. Each of us has his or her share of these dilemmas.

Just being a member of our modern society makes you a candidate for depression. If you can take the pace of life today without ever getting depressed you are exceptional. Most of us have our "down times."

A serious loss can trigger depression.

Often, depression follows a serious loss such as the death of a loved one, a divorce, retirement or bankruptcy. The loss of a lover, a friend, a job or the ability to have children can also trigger it. This type of depression is often referred to as a grief reaction.

Individuals, families, peer groups and as 9/11 taught us, even entire nations can be plunged into grief by common events we experience.

The ghastly onslaught of death and destruction evil terrorists heaped upon our nation draped a pall of depression across our whole nation. At this writing, people in the areas directly affected are still struggling to recover. Usually, the more unexpected and sudden our loss is, the longer our period of recovery will be.

Our work with people in crisis over the last 35 years indicates that regardless of how long the recovery period may be, it typically moves through four discernable stages. Although their sequence is distinguishable, each successive stage will overlap the previous one.

Stage 1. Shock

During this time, we are dazed. We feel like what we are going through is a bad dream or a nightmare. We expect to wake up and find it is not true. This usually lasts from several hours to a few days. However, in widespread disasters such as floods, fires, wars, terrorism, etc., weeks or even months may pass before the reality of it all sets in. But we finally realize that what we are experiencing is not a nightmare—it's true!

Stage 2. Storm

This is the most painful period of recovery. Our emotions are all over the place. Anxiety, fear, hostility and rage surge within us at almost unbearable levels. The storm phase of recovery lasts from several days to several weeks or even months.

3. Search

Once the emotional storm subsides we begin to search for some meaning to be found in our loss. We are driven to make sense of it all. During this time the one haunting question that hangs over us remains, "Where is God in all this?"

As tragic as the loss may be, this is not what we will live with; we will live with our memories of the loss. These memories are being built from stories we continue to tell ourselves about these events. The events will not repeat themselves, but our memories of them will. Satan wants our memories to be as destructive as possible. As overwhelming as the tragedy may be, Jesus wants to give us a creative way to live with our loss. Our search should not end until we find His creative version of our tragedy.

4. Sequel

As unbelievable as it may seem at the time, our life does go on after the loss. And the nature of that life will be determined largely by the ways we have chosen to remember our loss. What has happened to us can leave us bitter persons or better persons depending on who wins the battle for our memories. If our enemy wins we will be bitter. If our Lord wins we will be better!

A negative view of life can cause depression.

Unfortunately, some people are depressed because they have chosen to adopt a negative view of themselves and their world very early in life—long before they started to school. It is not their circumstances that depress them; it is their view of life.

From childhood they have chosen to see other people more favorably than themselves. Their value judgments are predictably negative. They are overly critical of themselves and others. They tend to see what is wrong about life rather than what is right.

Once I saw a cartoon of an old western town. The banner over the main street bore the name of the place. It was called– "Donut Center." Underneath the name, some kids had scrawled, "What a hole!" Some people choose to live there. We all spend a few days of our lives in such a place, but no one has to become a permanent resident. Remember this little limerick:

> As you journey through life,
> Let this be your goal:
> Keep your eye on the donut,
> And not on the hole!

How to deal with depression

Since we all come face to face with depression at one time or another here are some practical suggestions for dealing with it:

1. If you haven't had a thorough physical examination in the past six months, get one.

Even if nothing significant is found, at least you know that your depression is not symptomatic of some physical illness. Then, you can focus on the spiritual warfare necessary to put the most positive possible interpretation on the negative circumstances of your life.

2. Don't let the fact that you're depressed, get you down.

Fear of depression, or guilt over being depressed, will only add to your discomfort. Remember, depression tends to feed upon itself. You become more depressed by dwelling on the fact that you are depressed. Monitor your thought life carefully. Listen to what you are saying to yourself. Identify those *urges, fantasies, and ideas* that would drag you even deeper into depression as coming from Satan and minimize them as much as you can. Magnify those *urges, fantasies, and ideas* that give you hope. They are from the Lord.

3. Learn the therapy that comes from staying busy.

Unless your depression is severe, stay busy. Don't brood! You may not be able to escape your depression entirely, but don't feed it. Depression has a ravenous appetite. The more you feed it the bigger it grows. So, the worst thing a depressed person can do is to brood over being depressed. Resist the temptation to dawdle and day-dream. Plunge yourself into activities!

4. Once you know you are physically healthy, exercise regularly.

This is not only good for your body it is good for your mind. Exercising a half hour a day three times a week also will improve the quality of your sleep.

5. Discover the relief that comes from sharing your burden with the Lord in prayer.

Centuries ago David learned this secret. He wrote, *"Cast your cares on the Lord and he will sustain you..."*.[18] Read Psalms 58 and 59. Notice how openly David shares his feelings with the Lord. He doesn't pull any punches. He says it just like he feels it. This ability to share his uncensored feelings with the Lord is what earned David the coveted title of being "a man after God's own heart."[19] You and I need to learn from him. Feelings too risky to share with our friends can be safely shared with the Lord.

David even trusted God with rage provoked by his enemies. He cries, *"Break the teeth in their mouths, O God; tear out, O Lord, the fangs of the lions! Let them vanish like water that flows away; when they draw the bow, let their arrows be blunted. Like a slug melting away as it moves along, like a stubborn child, may they not see the sun."*[20] Can you imagine the relief that came to David as he emptied these feelings out before the Lord?

There is no attempt to cover up his bitterness and contempt for his enemies. He prays, *"Deliver me from evildoers and save me from bloodthirsty men .... They return at evening, snarling like dogs, and prowl about the city. See what they spew from their mouths—they spew out swords from their lips...For the sins of their mouths, for the words of their lips, let them be caught in their pride. For the curses and lies they utter, consume them in wrath, consume them till they are no more."*[21]

Learn to trust your vicious, angry, hostile feelings to God. There is nothing you feel that you can't express to Him. Find a private time and place for pouring your heart out to God. Never fear that an honest disclosure of your deepest feelings may alienate Him from you.

You may have felt that it is necessary to hide certain things from your parents or even your closest friend, but there is nothing you cannot share with your heavenly Father. God wants you to cast "all your care upon him."[22]

6. Share your burden with a friend.

Talking helps. My heart goes out to people who grew up in homes where children were to be seen and not heard. As adults, they are likely to be very private people who keep their feelings to themselves. When they were young they tried talking, but no one wanted to listen. So, now they are convinced that talking doesn't help. But it does!

Let me prove this to you. Suppose you and three of your friends got in your car and head home after a night of fellowship. As you approach the interstate you make your entry safely and start down the highway. At the first major intersection some fellow darts out in front of you.

You have to swerve off the road to miss him. You almost flip over. Now, what are the chances that you and your friends will go down the highway without making any comment about what happened?

Remember, there is no intellectual need to discuss what happened. You are all intelligent adults. Each of you saw everything that took place. None of you can add to the others' information. However, I'll venture that you wouldn't get a quarter-mile down the road until one of you would excitedly ask, *"Did you see that crazy idiot?"* From an intellectual point of view that is an absurd question. Of course, everyone in the car saw *"that crazy idiot."* But before that question would be answered someone else would anxiously observe, "Wow! We almost got it."

It's highly likely that you would continue to talk about your close call as you traveled down the road together. Probably, one of the first things you would say to your family after arriving home would be something like, "We almost didn't make it home. We were almost killed!"

Why would you carry on all this conversation if talking doesn't help? Well, the truth is, talking does help! It helps to reduce our level of anxiety. Sometimes it helps us look at our circumstances from a different and more positive perspective. It helps to lighten our burden. That's why Paul instructs us, *"Carry each other's burdens, and in this way you will fulfill the law of Christ."*[23]

When words are used as God intends them to be, they decrease our pain and increase our pleasure. Healthy conversation with yourself and a trusted friend can go a long way toward shortening the night of your depression and hastening the dawn of the new day you long to see.

Surviving deep depression

When depression is severe, a person may have to be relieved of all responsibilities. Notice how God treated

Elijah's suicidal level of depression. First of all, Elijah was temporarily relieved of all his responsibility. Today, such a goal is usually accomplished by hospitalizing the person. One of the primary benefits of hospitalizing the severely depressed person is to keep him safe and give him total rest.

Second, Elijah was put to sleep. Depressed people tend toward extremes in their sleep patterns. Some may not be able to go to sleep. Others may wake up frequently during the night, or they may waken an hour or two before their normal rising time and be unable to go back to sleep. On the other hand, some depressed people want to sleep most of the time. Of course, neither of these extremes is healthy. However, adequate sleep is part of any successful recovery program.

Third, diet was an important part of Elijah's treatment. A properly balanced diet is important in any recovery plan for depression.

Fourth, renewed spiritual vitality was at the heart of Elijah's treatment.[24] Any Christian who has been depressed understands how important spiritual renewal is to recovery.

Medication

New and better medications for depression are being developed. If these medications had been available to my wife they could have shortened that miserable period in her life. At EMERGE, our mental health center, we take a conservative view toward medication. Under competent medical supervision, however, we have found medication to be very helpful for people suffering from moderate to severe depression.

Often, depressed people are under the mistaken notion that the fewer pills they take the healthier they are. On the other hand, the longer they take medication the sicker they tend to see themselves. Nothing could be further from the truth. In fact, if they reduce their medication or cease to take it before they have recovered, their condition will very likely worsen. If medication is part of the treatment it is important that it be prescribed by a competent physician, taken according to his instructions, and terminated only under his supervision.

Celebrate every bright spiritual moment!

The Christian battling depression should celebrate every bright spiritual moment as evidence of God's involvement in the recovery process. The pattern of recovery for most people will involve a gradual emergence from depression. Little by little periods of relief will grow longer and more frequent. Periods of depression will become less frequent and less intense.

Long-range goals for the depression prone

Some Christians must have total success in every venture they undertake or they feel totally defeated. There is something to be said, however, for improvement in situations where total recovery may not be attainable. If you are a depression-prone person and would like to be as free from depression as possible, let me suggest some long-range goals for you. They may not eliminate depression in your future, but they can minimize the toll it takes on you.

1. See the advantages of depression.

For many people, depression is a primary way of coping with stress. Some people deal with stress in ways that damage their cardiovascular or gastrointestinal system. This can result in permanent damage to these vital organs. As painful as depression can be, once the misery of the mood has lifted, you are not as likely to have damaged your body as are those who manage stress in these other ways.

2. Creatively manage your angry feelings.

Often, a large component of depression is anger turned inwardly toward oneself. When Sue came to see me, she had been depressed during the Christmas holidays for years. She couldn't understand this. Sue and her husband had a good marriage. Their children were healthy. The family was full of love. They enjoyed being together.

Sue's depression, however, spoiled much of the joy of Christmas for the whole family. She wanted to do something about it, so we began to search for the source of her holiday depression.

Sue grew up in a large family. Her mother was an alcoholic. As a child she had dreamed of having a happy Christmas, but it never happened. Her mother was always drunk. There was no money for presents. Christmas was one of the unhappiest times of the year for her. She could remember thinking, "I hate my mother. If she wanted to, she could make Christmas nice for us—but she would rather get drunk."

Sue had never dealt with this anger. She needed to acknowledge it, to get it out of her. I encouraged Sue to forgive herself and to forgive her mother. Once these issues were dealt with, Sue and her family had their first depression-free Christmas.

When we are willing to acknowledge that anger plays a significant role in our depression we have gone a long way toward doing something constructive about it. See if you can identify what it is you are angry about. Then, go back to Chapter 5 and review the suggestions for managing your anger.

3. Work on adopting a positive worldview.

You can test the nature of your worldview by looking at the way you see the future. As a believer, what parts of Bible prophecy most intrigue you: the coming judgment, the antichrist, the mark of the beast, the battle of Armageddon, or the Millennium? A person with a positive view of the future assumes, "This world hasn't seen its best days yet, and neither have I!"

Here is Paul's thought filter for those who want to focus on the positive things in life. *"Finally, brothers, whatever is true, whatever is noble, whatever is right, whatever is pure, whatever is lovely, whatever is admirable—if anything is excellent or praiseworthy—think about these things."*[25]

4. See the divine potential in other people.

Learn the thrill of seeing God in the lives of your family members. See Him in the circumstances of your friends' lives. Of course, the powers of this world and Satan are at work, but we have the choice of where we fix our focus.

Having a positive view of life has nothing to do with closing your eyes to evil. You see it. You know it exists, but you don't choose to focus on it. You choose to focus on Christ *"because the one who is in you is greater than the one who is in the world."*[26]

Remember, Jesus is the door into another dimension of life. Don't be content merely to step out of an old life. Be determined to step into a new one. In the next chapter, I will share with you some of the exiting discoveries which await the Christian who is determined to explore this new dimension of life in Christ.

Discussion Questions

1. What are some of the reasons why the days in which we live might be referred to as the "age of depression."
2. What is depression?
3. What are some of its characteristics?
4. What affects does a person's self-image have on depression?
5. Who suffers from depression?
6. What are the four stages through which one will pass in recovering from grief?
7. How long does it take for one to recover from grief?
8. Why are people who take medication for other illnesses reluctant to take it for depression?
9. How does one's view of life affect his or her proneness to depression?
10. What are some important steps to take in dealing with depression?

FOOTNOTES

[1] Robins LN, Regier, DA (Eds). Psychiatric Disorders in America, The Epedemiologic Catchment Area Study, New York: The Free Press, 1990.

[2] Goleman, D. Emotional Intelligence. New York, NY: Bantam Books, 1997, p.240.

[3] Goleman, D. Emotional Intelligence. New York, NY: Bantam Books, 1997, p.240

[4] Goleman, D. Emotional Intelligence. New York, NY: Bantam Books, 1997, p.241.

[5] http://www.thebody.com/nimh/depressiondefeat.html, p.2 10/13/2002.

[6] Brokaw, Tom. The Greatest Generation, New York, NY: Random House, 1998, p.34.

[7] http://www.nimh.nih.gov/publicat/depression.cfm, p.2, 10/13/2002

[8] http://archfami.ama-assn.org/issues/v7n5/ffull/foc7016.html, 10/18/2002.

[9] http://www.thebody.com/nimh/depression_defeat..html, p.3, 10/13/2002

[10] http://www.nimh.nih.gov/publicat/depression.cfm, 10/13/2002, p.2.

[11] Job 2:13

[12] Job 3:2-4, 11

[13] Job 2:9

[14] Job 1:8

[15] Psalms 42:3

[16] I Kings 19:3, 4

[17] Matthew 26:75 (KJV)

[18] Psalms 55:22

[19] Acts 13:22

[20] Psalms 58:6-8

[21] Psalms 59:2, 6, 7, 12, 13

[22] I Peter 5:7

[23] Galatians 6:2

[24] I Kings 19:5-8

[25] Philippians 4:8

[26] I John 4:4

CHAPTER EIGHT

YOU CAN LIVE
IN A
NEW
DIMENSION

On our journey through this space-time world each of us has moments when we are aware of another reality lying just beyond our four-dimensional grasp. Like a subliminal shadow that hauntingly stalks, it reminds us of our lost paradise.

Perhaps this is what makes us so curious about paranormal phenomena. Even though we know these experiences are not scientifically verifiable most of us believe in them.

In the early 1960s Rod Serling capitalized on this eagerness to explore life in another dimension with his popular TV series, "The Twilight Zone."

Every week millions of Americans looked forward to being fascinated and frightened by each episode that began with him saying, "There is a fifth dimension beyond those known to man. It is a dimension vast as space and timeless as infinity. It is the middle ground between light and shadow, between the pit of his fears and the summit of his knowledge. This is the dimension of imagination. It is an area called the Twilight Zone."[1] When your friends thought you were getting too far out with your ideas, they began to hum the musical theme of this popular TV series to you.

We have all had our share of experiences with "woo-woo" people who live in their own spiritual twilight zone. However, aside from the "wackiness" of a few, many of us never discover the very real practical supernatural spiritual dimensions of our faith.

On September 11, 2001, al Qaeda terrorists came crashing through our limited version of reality. We were awakened in a startling and unforgettable way to the fact that there is an invisible spiritual dimension of reality that extends beyond our limited four-dimensional understanding of our planet.

This reality can only be depicted by such words as God, Satan, good and evil. Previously these words were considered to be "far out" by most people in the western world, but they have suddenly been restored to a respectable place in the conversations of our secular society.

The al Qaeda terrorist network, suicide bombers, snipers and others like them have cruelly scarred us with their uncanny ability to unleash their devastatingly destructive urges, fantasies and ideas, spawned in the evil power of their own imaginations, upon the innocent. To think that human beings could give physical expression to such evil urges, fantasies and ideas defies our wildest imagination. Behind their actions is a world of evil spirits where such shocking acts of terror are commonly conceived.

On the other hand, Christians today are challenged to believe that there is One in us who also wants to conceive urges, fantasies and ideas in our mental processes that will shock the world with practical physical expressions of His mind-defying goodness.[2] And we are assured that this One who is in us is greater than the evil one who is in this world.[3]

Making the supernatural practical

Much of my life has been spent searching for ways to make this supernatural dimension of reality practical for Christians. Science recognizes the power of the invisible and has taught us to respect it. The material secrets of the universe are hidden in the invisible forces of nature.

Seeking to know as much as possible about how the

universe began, our generation has peered farther back toward the creation of the universe than any other in the history of civilization. Some idea of the changes scientific discoveries have required my generation to make in our thinking can be seen in comparing what we were taught in high school with what the current generation is taught.

In my high school physics class we were taught the "billiard ball" atom theory. We learned that the atom was the smallest form of matter and it could not be divided. We were reminded that the English word "atom" has its roots in the Greek word "atomos" which means "indivisible."

As you know, in our lifetime the atom has been exploded so many times that nuclear physicists have found a whole universe of sub-atomic particles and are still looking for more. The universal world of the atom cannot be seen by the naked eye. Nevertheless, it contains the keys of life and death for our entire planet. In much the same way, the invisible spirit world holds the keys of good and evil in the world of matter.

The Scriptures teach that beyond the invisible dynamics of the physical sciences there is an unseen spiritual power responsible for creating and sustaining the universe.[4] John calls this Creator the Logos. He defines the power residing in Him and emanating from Him as *"zoe."*[5] This is the Greek word for "eternal life."

Over the last 35 years I have worked with thousands of Christians but have found very few aware of the practical daily benefits of having "eternal life." As Christians, we are more likely to think of eternal life as an existence that will begin for us when we die or when Jesus returns. Recently, I heard a well-intentioned preacher refer to a Christian who had died as "having entered into eternal life."

All of us look forward to being with the Lord.

However, He wants us to discover how this dynamic gift can enrich our *lives* now. He wants "eternal life" to be a prominent and practical part of our *present* life.

Many of us have not discovered how to relate this marvelous creative power to the practical decision-making, problem-solving challenges we face everyday.

Eternal life is creative and powerful.

Eternal life is the creative power God used in bringing the universe into existence. Here's how John says it happened, *"In the beginning was the Word, and the Word was with God, and the Word was God. He was with God in the beginning. Through him all things were made; without him nothing was made that has been made. In him was life; and that life was the light of men."*[6]

The Greek word translated "eternal life" in this passage is *zoe* not *bios*. *Bios* is the Greek word used 11 times in the New Testament to refer to natural life. However, the word *zoe* occurs 134 times in the New Testament and in 120 of these passages it refers to a kind of life that is obviously supernatural. *Zoe* is spiritual and invisible, but so powerful that the material universe is simply one of its manifestations. This creative power has always resided in and emanated from Jesus.[7] He is the source of this creative life, or energy. Everything in the universe has come from Him. And, God has given us this "eternal life" as His love gift to us in Jesus.[8]

Why did God send that love gift?

In the beginning, God created Adam and Eve capable of mentally interacting with this invisible creative power of life that emanated from Him. They communed with God every day[9]. Adam demonstrated the unusually creative dimension of thinking this life stimulated in his mind, by the way he carried out his appointed task of naming all the animals.[10]

When Adam chose to disobey God he could no longer be trusted with this life, so God denied him access to it.[11] Consequently, the part of Adam's mind capable of responding became dead in "trespasses and sins."[12] He suffered the loss of this whole creative dimension of thought. God warned him that this would happen if he chose to eat of the fruit from the forbidden tree.[13] So, Adam's state of spiritual death and his incapacity to respond to the life of God's presence has been transmitted to every human being since then. "In Adam all die."[14]

However, God's love for you and me is so great that to provide a way for us to be in communion with Him again He offered His Son to die for our sins so that the penalty for those sins could be justly satisfied.[15] When we accepted Christ's death and resurrection as an atonement for our sins we experienced a new birth that makes us members of a "new creation."[16]

What part of us is born again?

The part of us that is born again is that part of our spirit or mind that became dead to God's creative life when Adam sinned. This is why theologians refer to the "new birth" as "regeneration." Through the "new birth" our spirit that was insensitive to God is regenerated or brought back to life. Subsequently, we are capable of communing with God and responding to the eternal life that emanates from Christ just like Adam was able to commune with God before he disobeyed and fell into sin.

Our regenerated sensitivity to eternal life enables us to experience the love of the Father, the triumphant presence of the Son, and the teaching ministry of the Holy Spirit. So, when we are born again *"zoe"* quickens our spirit. This eternal life begins to "stimulate our brain to think in terms of urges, fantasies and ideas that enhance and develop our divine potential." We are alive and sensitive to the presence of God. We can commune with Him, and He with us.

Divine options for problem solving and decision making that would otherwise remain obscure to us become obvious. However, our spirit is also still sensitive to sin as it "impacts our mind stimulating our brain to think in terms of urges, fantasies and ideas that detract from and destroy our divine potential." We become aware of a war that is being waged in our mental activity.[17]

Thinking is *always* spiritual warfare!

Many of us have trouble relating the invisible power of sin and eternal life to the practical issues of our daily lives. We struggle with knowing how to identify these divine options in our thoughts when we are faced with critical parental decisions. How can we access this kind of creativity in resolving out marital conflict? How do we access these creative ideas when we face the challenges of the work place?

Many of us have difficulty understanding how to apply the spiritual dimensions of our mental activity to practical issues like this.

Thinking is so common we assume it to be a totally natural activity. We take a giant stride toward living in a new dimension when we become aware of the supernatural dimension that is always active in our thought processes. Both temptations for expressing evil and divine suggestions for expressing good are supernatural in origin. Yet, they come to us through the same kinds of urges, fantasies, and ideas we usually associate with our natural thought processes.

Remember, temptations are the product of an invisible *supernatural* power emanating from Satan. And, divine suggestions that are stimulated in our urges, fantasies and ideas result from an invisible *supernatural* power emanating from Jesus Christ.

Unfortunately, our fallen nature makes us more aware of temptations than we are of divine suggestions. We tend to be so inattentive to divine suggestions God endeavors to stimulate in our thoughts that moments when we are overwhelmed by temptations create uncomfortable levels of guilt and anxiety in us.

A practical understanding of the power of eternal life and its daily presence in our decision making process can eliminate much of this anxiety. Remember, there is always a supernatural dimension in our mental activity and so we need to be more aware of it.

Eternal life is not magic!

Eternal life is an invisible supernatural power, but it is not magic. In fact, the supernatural is neither magical nor superstitious. It is another dimension of reality in which God does His work at levels of understanding beyond our comprehension.[18]

Once we become aware of the impact of eternal life on our thought processes, God will involve us with Him in the miracles needed in our lives. Paul says it this way: *"...continue to work out your salvation with fear and trembling, for it is God who works in you both to will and to act according to his good purpose."*[19] The fact that we are involved makes what happens in our lives no less supernatural. Paul assures us of this: *"Now to him who is able to do immeasurably more than all we ask or imagine, according to his power that is at work in us."*[20]

How can we be more aware of the supernatural?

God wants to guide each of us in the critical decisions of our daily lives. Paul assures us of this, because

"those who are led by the Spirit of God are sons of God."[21]
Through creative prayer we can become increasingly aware
of the spiritual activity in our mental processes. As our
awareness of this activity grows, God will help us develop
a growing ability to know the difference between those
urges, fantasies and ideas resulting from sin and those orig-
inating from eternal life and, others suggested by our own
natural thought processes.

Scripture stored in our memory becomes an invaluable tool in discerning the spiritual origin of our urges, fantasies and ideas.[22] We will become more skilled in our discernment with practice and experience.[23]

Prayer is the key!

Prayer is one of the most misunderstood of all spiritual activities. Many of us see prayer as a time of pleading
with God to act on our behalf. If this is the way we see
prayer then we are more likely to pray when we need protection or some other divine favor. For us, prayer easily
can become a way we believe we can get God to do what
we want Him to do. In fact, some of us make lists to be
sure we don't forget anything. And when God doesn't do
what we want Him to do, when we want Him to do it, we
often get angry with Him.

Sometimes a person will say to me, "I'm not going
to pray anymore because prayer doesn't work." When I
ask him or her to explain what he or she means, he or she
often express great disappointment that God did not do
what he or she asked Him to do. People who see prayer
like this seem to blame God for the bad things that happen
to them—and the good things that don't.

God does want us to bring our requests to him, but
this is such a small part of what prayer is all about.[24]
Mature believers see prayer as a way of learning what God
wants us to do for Him rather than telling Him what we

want Him to do for us.[25] How sad for those who never make this discovery.

Trust God for your material needs!

God wants us to learn to trust Him for our material needs so more of our prayer time can be devoted to seeking and exploring His kingdom. Jesus teaches us that the material things we need will come to us as by-products of putting His kingdom first in our lives.

Here are the priorities He urges us to pursue in our prayers: *"So do not worry saying, 'What shall we eat?' Or 'What shall we drink?' or 'What shall we wear?' For the pagans run after all these things, and your heavenly Father knows you need them. But seek first the kingdom and his righteousness, and all these things will be given to you as well. Therefore do not worry about tomorrow, for tomorrow will worry about itself. Each day has enough trouble of its own."*[26]

Prayer is more than words we say. Prayer is the ongoing communion of our Spirit with God's Spirit throughout the activities of the day.[27] It is an attitude of the heart that opens our mind or spirit to new creative ways God wants to show us for approaching the problem-solving, decision-making challenges of life. This is praying without ceasing.

What is creative praying?

Creative praying is based on the assumption that invisible spiritual powers are at least as active in shaping the events of our world as invisible natural powers—and just as predictable in the ways they operate.[28] Yet the idea of an invisible power - eternal life - making a significant daily impact on the decisions we make and the way we solve our problems sounds so mystical to some.[29]

Because we have discovered the technology that

reveals the power of an electro-magnetic field, the wind, a vacuum, electricity and can harness these invisible natural powers for practical use in our daily lives, we believe in them. But they are no more visible than the invisible powers of the spiritual world.

Just as science has discovered invisible sources of natural power and put them to practical use, so the Bible defines the principles and properties of *sin* and *eternal life* and explains how they function in our world. By tapping into Biblical truth we can gain an understanding of these powers and learn how to relate them to the practical issues of our daily lives. Through prayer and study of Scriptures we can learn how *sin* and *eternal life* affect our thought processes and the choices that shape our destinies. Why should it be so difficult for us to believe in these invisible mental stimuli when the invisible forces of nature are such a commonly accepted part of our life?

Then, creative praying is based on the belief that spirit is more powerful than matter. Spirit preceded matter in existence. All matter has come from spirit.[30] Matter is temporal. It has a beginning and an ending. God is eternal and supreme over all. Creative praying keeps us continually aware of this.

Why should a person engage in creative praying?

1. Creative prayer helps to make us a new creation.

Through creative praying children of Adam become children of God.[31] We never pray a more creative prayer than when we ask God to forgive our sins and enable us to be born again.

Acknowledging our personal need of Christ's atonement not only makes it possible for our sins to be forgiven; it also enables us to become aware of and sensitive to eternal life.[32] This new awareness makes us conscious of the difference between the urges, fantasies, and ideas stimulated in our mind by Satan and those stimulated by Christ. With this awareness comes a desire to live out those urges, fantasies, and ideas stimulated in us by Christ while denying expression to those stimulated in us by Satan. This is what the process of "putting off the old man" and "putting on the new man" is all about. Paul calls this being "renewed in the spirit of your mind."[33]

2. Creative prayer changes the way you view your past.

When you are born again the hurts of your past are not always automatically and instantly healed. Being born again is the initial treatment of an ailing life; it is not the total cure.

Many of us bring into our Christian life unpleasant memories that have left deep and painful scars on us. Such old hurts need to be healed so that we do not unconsciously—or perhaps, consciously—cling to all their pain. Unless we surrender old hurts to Christ, they can cripple us and get in the way of the future He has for us.

Although the facts of our personal history remain fixed, we can change the way we choose to feel and think about those facts. We don't have to be a prisoner of our past.

I talk to many people who battle bitterness, anger, fear, jealousy, disappointments, or other damaging feelings. Often, such pain has its roots in what happened in our families, marriages, job situations, or church squabbles. We may feel our parents abused or mistreated us, our brothers and sisters were unfair to us, a former mate took advantage of us, a business partner cheated us, or people in the church gossiped about us. These are the kinds of things that can fester in our spirit and poison our life. Pains from our past can spill over into our present and cast dark shadows on our future. God wants us to discover creative ways of viewing them!

3. Creative prayer changes the way you view your world.

It is amazing how different our external world looks once our internal world of memories has been healed. Many problems with others simply disappear. As you have probably noticed, problems between people usually have their roots in problems within people.

Washing your own windows helps!

Years ago, when people hung their washing outside to dry, a lady was always complaining about how dirty her neighbor's clothes were. Then one day, she washed her windows and became amazed at how clean her neighbor's clothes had become. The internal perspective from which you view your world affects the way you see it.

When Moses brought Israel to the edge of the Promised Land some people saw it as a land full of tall giants that made them feel like grasshoppers. Others saw it as a land full of milk and honey and were confident they could conquer it.[34] A healthy person learns to view the harsh realities of life as positively as possible. God gives these creative vantage points to us during times of prayer and meditation. He helps us see our circumstances in the most positive possible way.

4. Creative prayer helps change the external realities of life.

God seldom performs miracles that affect us without involving us. Jesus changed the water into wine, but first the servants filled the water pots with water.[35] I see many people who want God to do a miracle for their marriage or their family, but they don't want to assume any responsibility for changing their circumstances.

These people usually blame their unhappiness on others—their parents, their brothers and sisters, their friends, their mates, their former mates, their children, the devil. The list is endless. In their eyes, they are not responsible for what has happened to them and they are not able to do anything about it. Only God can deliver them!

This kind of passive-dependent person is a bystander in life! Someone has said there are basically three kinds of people in the world: people who make things happen, people who watch things happen, and people who never quite figure out what is happening!

Passive-dependent people never seem to get out of the grandstand of their own lives. Usually these people are frightened of life and angry at others for not doing more to help them. They see their problems as the work of the devil. They insist that only the Lord can solve their problems. Satan causes them and Jesus takes them away while they themselves remain passive during the whole magical process.

God honors those who see Him in their struggles.

Donna discovered the secrets of this spiritual dimension when she was facing impossible odds in her struggle for survival. When I first met her she was single, in her teens and living in a wheelchair. The doctors gave her little hope of becoming an adult. She had suffered polio as a child, and this was working against her in an apparently losing battle she was waging with tuberculosis. Her family had called me to the hospital.

As I approached Donna's bedside, before I could even greet her, she announced to me, "The doctors say I'm gonna die." Then she added, "It's not their fault. They're doing the best they can to save my life." "What do you think about what the doctors have told you?" I asked. "I think they're wrong," she said with a twinkle in her eye. I spent a few minutes affirming her faith, had prayer with her and left.

This was the first of many trips I made to the hospital during Donna's battle with tuberculosis. That was over 30 years ago, and she is still going strong.

Her doctors provided her the best treatment possible, but they were wrong in their prognosis. They also discouraged her from getting married, and told her she could never give birth to a child. They were wrong again.

In a day when some able-bodied people have difficulty finding one suitable mate, Donna found two. Her first husband loved her very much. He took care of her as long as he lived. They had two lovely children: a son and a daughter. Both are grown and married. Today, Donna is a grandmother.

A few years after her first husband died, Donna met and married another man who thinks the sun rises and sets on her. The last time I saw her, she was at a church where I was speaking. After the service we had a few moments to reminisce. "Donna," I said, "the first time I saw you I didn't think you were going to make it."

"I know," she responded with a chuckle. "You were just like the rest of those doctors. But I fooled you, didn't I?" "You sure did," I admitted. "Now, if somebody told me you were dead, I wouldn't believe them." "Well, it's just the Lord," Donna said humbly. "He's the one. He's brought me through."

That's the truth. God opened a new dimension of life for Donna that the medical world knew very little about. Living in that dimension she found the hope and faith that brought healing in her life. Of course, Donna also played a role in her own survival. God opened the door, but she had to walk through it.

Focusing on the spiritual power of faith enabled Donna to rise above the clumsiness of her crippled body. She refused to be dominated by her emotions. After all, for much of her life they would have given her little to feel good about. Most of the time, Donna's spirit has been in the driver's seat of her life and the Lord has been her driving instructor.

The Lord wants you to be in this elite group with Donna. He wants to put you in the driver's seat of your own life, and you can count on Him to be your driving instructor. He'll keep you focused on your final destination and won't let you wander off on tempting shortcuts or costly detours. He will stimulate in you urges, fantasies, and ideas that will help you *"will and act according to his good purpose."*[36]

God never asks us to do what He knows we can't. As we put the possible in His hand, He uses it in doing the impossible. When Moses stretched out his rod toward the Red Sea, God parted the water.[37] When Israel was willing to march around the walls of Jericho, God tore them down.[38] When one lad gave the Lord his five loaves and two fish, Jesus fed 5000 men plus the women and children.[39]

People who just want to pray and let God do it all are exposing themselves to the risk of devastating disappointments.

Prayer alone seldom changes things.

Prayer usually changes people—and people change things. Don't misunderstand. God can do all things. However, He has chosen us to become *"workers together with him."*[40]

By engaging in creative prayer, ordinary people like you and I can learn how to be involved with God in extraordinary manifestations of eternal life in our world.

How do you pray creatively?
First, commit God's Word to memory.

God delights in us memorizing Scripture. I try to store up a few new verses each year. David found that hiding God's Word in his heart helped him build up an internal resistance to destructive attitudes and habits that sin tried to generate in his life.[41]

Second, spend time listening in prayer.

Prayer can be an exercise in one-way communication. Some of us do all the talking and expect God to do all the listening and obeying. When we are finished talking to God, we are finished praying. Yet, often in Scripture we are instructed to wait on God and to listen for God to speak to us.[42]

At first, when we start to listen in prayer we may find it difficult to hear. So, let me suggest you begin by determining that you will spend half of your prayer time in listening. Just make that a standard practice of your prayer life. For example, if you are in the habit of spending ten minutes a day in prayer, then spend the first five minutes talking to God and the last five minutes letting Him talk to you.

When you begin to develop the art of listening in prayer, don't be surprised to discover a thousand voices filling the silence. The worries of yesterday, the cares of today, the fears of tomorrow will try to come crashing in on you. Keeping a note book near may be helpful in preserving those insights and suggestions the Lord gives you in moments of prayer. This practice not only provides you a journal or "to do" list, but writing will also free you from distractions that so easily break into your concentration when you are praying.

Practice is essential if you are to develop this spiritual skill. In time the Lord will help you to become proficient in taking "captive every thought to make it obedient to Christ.[43]

We lead a noisy life.

Americans are conditioned to a noisy life. When we wake up in the morning we turn on the radio or television to get our morning noise. In fact, some of us are wakened by the radio.

Many of us cannot stand the stillness in our automobiles. No sooner do we get in the car and crank up the engine than we turn on the radio; or, we get on the telephone.

The last thing turned off at night in many homes is the radio or television. So, from the time we get out of bed in the morning until we crawl back into bed at night, many of us are more comfortable with noise than with silence.

Even in our churches there is very little silence. The organ is playing. Someone is singing. Someone is making announcements. The preacher is speaking. Many of us are so unaccustomed to silence in worship that we would find it extremely awkward. We may assume it to be an indication of spiritual death.

God wants us to seek out some quiet time. He urges us to develop the ability to listen to what the Spirit would say to us.

We are bombarded with stimuli from waking to sleeping. Mental fatigue is common among us. Consequently, often our ability to distinguish trivia from issues essential to our relationships is impaired. Millions of sights and sounds compete for our attention every day. Many of us are mentally tired, even when our bodies are rested.

Few have learned how to rest their mind. One way of doing this is to develop the art of listening in prayer. Nothing is more restful and refreshing than quiet time before God. The psalmist learned this. The Lord taught him: *"Be still, and know that I am God."*[44]

Isaiah discovered, *"They that wait upon the Lord shall renew their strength; they shall mount up with wings as eagles; they shall run, and not be weary; and they shall walk and not faint."* [45]

Third, wait upon the Lord!

Meditation is one of the oldest forms of Christian worship and prayer. Although western Christianity has neglected this ancient tradition of the church, other religions are using it effectively as a means of attracting mentally tired Americans through the serenity that meditation offers.

Today, meditation is associated with Eastern religions so often that some are reluctant to practice it. But God wants His people to enjoy the benefits of meditation. David describes the "blessed" or happy man as one whose, *"delight is in the law of the Lord; and on his law he meditates day and night."*[46] Some of the most creative moments of my life have come as I have sat quietly to listen to Him speak to me through His Spirit and from His Word after I have talked to Him, praised Him, worshipped Him and thanked Him.

Once you have developed the ability to wait and listen, you won't want to pray without some time for meditation. For years, I have found greater blessing in spending more time listening than talking in prayer.

If you are a beginner in learning to pray creatively, let me suggest that you take the first two or three minutes of your prayer time for quiet praise. Then, spend the next three or four minutes talking to God about your concerns. After that, rest your mind by committing all your cares to Jesus.[47] Focus your thoughts on a peaceful Bible scene or a restful verse of Scripture and wait quietly before the Lord. Learn to take advantage of those unplanned moments that come to you through the day by using them as opportunities for meditation.

For example, sometimes I wake up at 5:30 or 6 in the morning. I already have the hours of sleep I require. What am I going to do? I have several options. I can begin to wonder why it is that I can't go back to sleep. I can become very upset and frustrated because someone or something has disturbed me early in the morning and robbed me of my sleep. Or, I can take advantage of this unexpected quiet time in the presence of the Lord and listen for what He may want to say to me.

Often in such moments the Lord will remind me of people who need prayer. Or, He may bring to my attention certain situations I need to take care of and help me see them in ways I had not discovered. With these new perspectives the Lord also may suggest options for problem-solving that I had not thought of before. The wisdom He brings to us in creative moments like these makes our wisest thoughts appear foolish.

At such times the Lord may show you new ways to feel and think about some old hurts in your own life. He may help you change your views about people and events in your past which have caused you pain.

"Creative prayer can heal wounded relationships!"

It was during such a sleepless night that God healed Jacob of the ill feelings he had toward Esau.[48] Jacob was one of those people who believed that his troubles were caused by others. As he was coming back from his uncle Laban's, he remembered that he would soon meet his brother Esau. It had been years since the two had seen each other.

The last time Jacob was with his brother, Esau threatened to kill him. Jacob had collaborated with their mother, Rebecca, in swindling Isaac's blessing from Esau.

You can understand Esau's outrage when he discovered what had happened. Jacob believed Esau had kept that grudge alive for 14 years.

So, Jacob concocted an elaborate scheme to make peace with his brother. He sent animals to Esau. Then he strategically arranged his servants, his wives, and even his children in a spectacular parade of appeasement. Each group had a carefully-prepared speech designed to convince Esau that Jacob considered himself to be Esau's servant.

Even after he had organized this gigantic parade, Jacob was still so afraid that he sneaked off to spend the night on the other side of the brook. During the night God sent an angel to confront him. Jacob wrestled with the angel all night. As the dawn of Jacob's dreaded day began to break, the angel protested, *"Let me go."*

Jacob, afraid for his life, gripped the angel and cried, *"I will not let you go unless you bless me."*

The angel responded by asking Jacob to recall his name. Jacob was asked to honestly reflect on what defined him as a person. What had people come to expect from him? This question forced Jacob to face the real source of his problems for the first time in his life. He could no longer blame them on his father, his mother, his brother, or his uncle. He had to confront the fact that he was what his name implied—a deceiver. After that night, Jacob finally faced the real source of his troubles—himself. He would never be the same again. Even his name was changed.

Notice what happened the next day when he faced Esau. Esau threw his arms around Jacob and kissed him. Jacob discovered he had needlessly carried these fears and anxieties for years.

Esau had put those painful differences that divided them behind him. It was Jacob who had harbored the grudge and kept it alive in his mind. Just think of the needless torture he had heaped upon himself!

Ever since the fall of Adam we have tended to identify our own problems—but in other people. Children blame their problems on their parents. When divorce tears up a marriage, both partners tend to believe their divorce was mostly due to their mate's shortcomings or misbehavior. When people are fired, they accuse management of being unfair.

Of course, there are those instances in life where others are the source of our problems. However, often God must help us see that the problems we have with others are largely of our own making. And, the changes which need to take place are mostly within us.

Creative prayer helps in problem solving.

Creative prayer can help us discover new alternatives for solving the problems confronting us. It can also help us define new options for decisions we have to make.

While you are meditating begin to define the options your own wisdom and experience suggest. In your imagination, project each of these options, one at a time, far enough into the future to anticipate their ultimate consequences.

Often, the Holy Spirit will give us a fascination for an option we have defined through this process. At other times, He will stimulate another option through the creative power of eternal life, an option that had not previously occurred to us.

How will we know the difference between foolish thoughts that may surface during these moments of meditation and creative ways our regenerated mind may suggest we view our situation? That distinction can be made more simply than you may imagine.

First of all, suggestions stimulated by eternal life are always consistent with Scripture.

Second, options stimulated by eternal life will improve our relationships with the significant people in our life. God will never lead us to do anything that would destroy our marriage or family. He will never lead us to do anything that would embarrass the body of Christ. He will never prompt us to be harmful to our neighbors or ourselves. Any suggestions eternal life may introduce will be consistent with the most redemptive and creative possible ways of approaching the circumstances and relationships of our life.

Third, divine suggestions will lend themselves to making us more effective in doing what God has called us to do. God is glorified when we excel in the expression of the gifts and talents He has given us.

Fourth, whatever eternal life suggests is practical. It works! Often, when wisdom finally surfaces it is so obviously appropriate that we wonder why we didn't think of it sooner. However, never let the practicality of a creative suggestion diminish your appreciation for its supernatural origin.

Some people can only see God in the spectacular. At times He does move in spectacular ways, but more often He moves through the regular channels of the routine matters of our lives. As we develop an appreciation for God's guidance in the practical issues of our lives we will be excited to discover how frequently we find Him there.

You can sort it all out!

It takes practice to develop skill in sorting out divine suggestions from the stream of our own thoughts. And, in the process you may do a foolish thing or two. Most of us do, but be patient with yourself. After all, making a few mistakes is a small price to pay for the thrill of experiencing divine guidance in our lives.

The author of Hebrews reminds us that there is the

promise of growing skill in discernment with practice.[49] We become increasingly skilled in knowing the difference between those thoughts that result from confusion in and around us, those that are the products of sin, and those that are the creative voice of eternal life guiding us God's way.

A new dimension of living for you!

If you are still suffering from yesterday's hurts, then during prayer's quiet creative moments let the Lord show you healing ways to view your past. Nothing that has happened in the past needs to get in the way of God's best for your future.

I challenge you to become aware of the activity of eternal life in your thought processes. The resources with which we face our tomorrows are not limited to the options of our own mind. Remember, we have access to the mind of Christ which makes the wisdom of man look like foolishness.[50] Learning to draw from these resources in making major life decisions is a practical expression of walking in the Spirit.

Look at prayer differently than you have before. Begin to spend at least as much time listening to God as you spend talking to Him. Learn to identify the voice of the Lord in your thoughts. Involve His options in your problem-solving situations. The decision-making opportunities of our tomorrows can be more exciting and challenging for us as we learn how to become involved with the Lord in the process of discovering His will. In those creative moments you have with Him, sharpen your skills in hearing what he is saying to you. And, learn to do whatever He says.[51] As you do, you will find yourself celebrating life in a new dimension.

Discussion Questions

1. How does prayer serve as a doorway to living in a *new dimension?*

2. What is *eternal life?*

3. How can eternal life affect our life on earth?

4. What is sin?

5. How can it be recognized in our mental activity?

6. What are the steps involved in *creative prayer*

7. How does *creative prayer* help to heal painful memories and broken relationships?

8. What are some guidelines for helping a person distis-guish the difference between the urges, fantasies, and ideas stim-ulated by sin and those stimulated by *eternal life?*

9. How does one improve his or her skills in identifying the spiritual origin or urges, fantasies, and ideas?

10. What areas of your life can be helped by *creative prayer?*

FOOTNOTES

[1] The Columbia World of Quotations. Copyright © 1996 Columbia University Press, No. 49032.

[2] Matthew 5:16

[3] I John 1:4

[4] Colossians 12:15-17

[5] John 1:4

[6] John 1:1-3

[7] I John 5:11, 12

[8] John 3:16, 17

[9] Genesis 3:8

[10] Genesis 2:19, 20

[11] Genesis 3:24

[12] Ephesians 2:1

[13] Genesis 2:15-17

[14] I Corinthians 15:22

[15] Romans 5:12-21; 1 Peter 3:18

[16] 2 Corinthians 2:17

[17] Romans 7:21-25

[18] Isaiah 55:7-9

[19] Philippians 2:12, 13

[20] Ephesians 3:20

[21] Romans 8:14

[22] Hebrews 4:12

[23] Hebrews 5:11-14

[24] Philippians 4:6, 7

[25] Philippians 2:13

[26] Matthew 6:31-34

[27] I Thessalonians 5:16

[28] Hebrews 11:3

[29] Colossians 1:15-17

[30] John 1:1-3

[31] John 1:12

[32] Romans 6:11

[33] Ephesians 4:23

[34] Numbers 13:27,30,33

[35] John 2:1-11

[36] Philippians 2:13

[37] Exodus 14:21,22

[38] Joshua 6:6-20

[39] Matthew 14:15-21

[40] 2 Corinthians 6:1

[41] Psalms 119:11

[42] Revelation 2:7; Luke 8:18

[43] 2 Corinthians 10:5

[44] Psalms 46:10 (KJV)

[45] Isaiah 40:31(KJV)

[46] Psalms 1:2

[47] I Peter 5:7

[48] Genesis 32

[49] Hebrews 5:14

[50] I Corinthians 2:16

[51] John 2:5